GUNNAR MYRDAL

GARLAND REFERENCE LIBRARY
OF THE SOCIAL SCIENCES
(VOL. 125)

GUNNAR MYRDAL

Photo for "Les Prix Nobel en 1974" by Esbjörn Eriksson

GUNNAR MYRDAL
A Bibliography, 1919–1981

Kerstin Assarsson-Rizzi
Harald Bohrn

Second Edition, revised and enlarged by Kerstin Assarsson-Rizzi

GARLAND PUBLISHING, INC. • NEW YORK & LONDON
1984

Library of Congress Cataloging in Publication Data

Assarsson-Rizzi, Kerstin, 1944–
   Gunnar Myrdal, a bibliography, 1919–1981.

   (Garland reference library of social science ; no. 125)
   Rev. ed. of: Gunnar Myrdal, a bibliography, 1919–
1981 / by Harald Bohrn.
   Bibliography: p.
   Includes index.
   1. Myrdal, Gunnar, 1898– —Bibliography.
2. Economics—Bibliography. I. Bohrn, Harald, 1904–
II. Title. III. Series.
Z7164.E2M972 1984 [HB179.S8]   016.33   83-8944
ISBN 0-8240-9256-2

Printed on acid-free, 250-year-life paper
Manufactured in the United States of America

CONTENTS

PREFACE
TO THE SECOND EDITION

In bringing the bibliography of Professor Gunnar Myrdal's writings, first published in 1976, up to date, I have taken the opportunity to correct some errors and misprints. Furthermore, going through some of the material, I have been able to add some previously unnoticed pieces to the list. This does not mean, however, that completion has been achieved. The formidable task of compiling an exhaustive listing of Gunnar Myrdal's vast production in its many shapes and forms has not been within the scope of the present undertaking. Thus the reservations with which the original edition was brought out remain valid also for this edition. To the restrictions mentioned by Harald Bohrn I would like to add that no attempt has been made to record new printings of earlier publications.

The arrangement is that of the first edition. Additional books, articles and interviews, predating 1975, are listed at the end in a separate number sequence, and are followed by an errata list. It is hoped that the index, which has been entirely revised, will facilitate the finding of this new material.

Alva and Gunnar Myrdal's papers are housed in the Archives and Library of the Swedish Labour Movement, Box 1124, S-111 81 Stockholm. The collection is being organized by Stellan Andersson whose great familiarity with the material and kind assistance make it a pleasure to visit the Archives.

Professor Myrdal has been most helpful throughout the preparation of the new edition, as has Mrs. Caroline Burton. To both I would like to express my gratitude.

KERSTIN ASSARSSON-RIZZI
Stockholm in September 1981

INTRODUCTION

This is a bibliography with many reservations. Hardly any bibliography can be said to be complete. With regard to Professor Gunnar Myrdal's vast production, the incompleteness is not only inevitable but also, I'm afraid, extensive, since he has collaborated in publications which have appeared all over the world and which are not always easily available. Moreover, his major as well as his minor works have been published in the most varying shapes and forms. Of some categories, such as newspaper articles, addresses, forewords, opening speeches, opening statements, and interviews, only a few items have been included put at my disposal by Professor Myrdal himself. An attempt at completeness would have been too time-consuming, uncertain and haphazard. Naturally, the main stress has been laid on the author's scholarly activities, whereas political statements and contributions to the political and social debate have taken second place or been excluded. Stencilled papers have been included only in exceptional cases. The same thing applies to papers with incomplete bibliographical details. Unfortunately, it has not been possible to avoid a lack of consistency in listing the works. Nevertheless, this bibliography is the outcome of the collaboration of many people and institutions: libraries and archives, the editorial offices of journals and newspapers, publishing houses and private persons inside and outside Sweden, foreign embassies in Sweden and Swedish embassies abroad, etc. Since a specification would take up too much space, I shall have to confine myself—without mentioning any names—to tendering my warm and sincere thanks to all those who have so readily facilitated my work. Above all, of course, my thanks are due to Professor Myrdal himself, without whose interest and co-operativeness this bibliography would never have been completed.

The bibliography is chronological. The author's annual production is listed, where the material makes this possible, in two sections: first separate works and articles from journals, then (1) forewords, (2) newspaper articles, and (3) interviews. The two sections are separated by a horizontal line. The bibliography is concluded with an index.

HARALD BOHRN

Gunnar Myrdal

BIBLIOGRAPHY

+ indicates more important initial publications
* before title denotes joint authorship
The figures within brackets refer to entry numbers, not page numbers.

1919

1 Modern studentkultur. Stockholms studenter och de ideella intressena. [University Students and Their Culture in Our Time. The Students in Stockholm and the Idealistic Interests.] (Svenska Dagbladet 6/5 1919.) [Identical with 2. Cf. 3.]
Contribution to a debate signed "G.M., student 1918".

2 Studentens "idélöshet" och "gulaschmoral". Några reflexioner i ett aktuellt spörsmål. [The Student's "Lack of Ideas" and "Profiteer Morals". Some Reflections on a Question of the Moment.] (Lunds Dagblad 6/5 1919.) [Identical with 1. Cf. 3.]
Contribution to a debate signed "G.M., student 1918".

3 Studentkulturens höjande. En kollektiv meningsyttring från de yngre. [The Improvement of the Students' Culture. A Collective Manifestation from the Younger People.] (Svenska Dagbladet 17/5 1919.) [Cf. 1—2.]
Signed by G[unnar] M[yrdal]; F[ritz] T[horén]; B[ertil] L[öfström]; J[osef] A[lmquist]; B[ertil] K[arth]; S[ven] T[isell], "studenter 1918 och 1917". — The article was written by Gunnar Myrdal.

1927

4+ Prisbildningsproblemet och föränderligheten. Akad. avh. [Price Formation and the Change Factor. Doctoral dissertation.] Uppsala & Stockholm, Almqvist & Wiksell, 1927, 254 pp. (Ekonomisk Skriftserie 1.)

1928

5 Lantbrukets bristande räntabilitet. [The Insufficient Profitability of Agriculture.] (Svensk Tidskrift 18 (1928), pp. 463—476.)

1

1929

6 Folket och samhällsklasserna. [The People and the Classes of Society.] (Herlitz, Nils: Svensk samhällslära. Under medverkan av Gunnar Myrdal. Stockholm 1929, pp. 11—13.) [Cf. 22.]

7 Samhällsrörelser och organisationer. [Social Movements and Organizations.] (Herlitz, Nils: Svensk samhällslära, Under medverkan av Gunnar Myrdal. Stockholm 1929, pp. 13—23.) [Cf. 27.]

8[+] Sparandets plats i realinkomstberäkning. [The Place of Savings in Calculation of Real Income.] (Ekonomisk Tidskrift 31 (1929): 4, pp. 157—169.)

9 Staten och det ekonomiska livet. [The State and the Economic Life.] (Herlitz, Nils: Svensk samhällslära. Under medverkan av Gunnar Myrdal. Stockholm 1929, pp. 98—100.) [Cf. 30.]

1930

10 Alkoholens vinst- och förlustkonto. [Profit and Loss of Alcohol.] (Tirfing 24 (1930): 4, pp. 106—109.)

11a[+]Vetenskap och politik i nationalekonomien. [Later English title: The Political Element in the Development of Economic Theory.] Stockholm, Norstedt, 1930, 308 pp.
Adaptation of the author's lectures at the University of Stockholm in spring, 1928.

11b — Ny omarb. uppl. [New, rev. ed.] ... Stockholm 1971. (826)

11c Translations.
[English:] The Political Element in the Development of Economic Theory. London 1953. (228)
[—] — Cambridge, Mass., 1954. (233)
[—] — New York 1969. (715)
[German:] Das politische Element in der nationalökonomischen Doktrinbildung. Berlin 1932. (26)
[—] — Hannover 1963. (399)

2

[Greek:] To politiko stoicheio stēn oikonomikē theōria. Athēnai 1971. (A31)
[Italian:] L'elemento politico nella formazione delle dottrine
dell'economia pura. Firenze 1943. (111)
[—] L'elemento politico nello sviluppo della teoria economica. Firenze 1981. (1116)
[Japanese:] Keizai-gakusetsu to seijiteki yōso. Tōkyō [1942].
(102)
[—] — Tōkyō 1967. (570)
[Korean:] Kyŏngje haksŏl-kwa chŏngch'ijŏk yoso. Seoul.
1974. (A35)
[Spanish:] El elemento político en el desarrollo de la teoría
económica. Madrid 1967. (565)

1931

12 Diskriminering av räntan. Svar på anmärkningarna [&]
Slutreplik [till Anders Örne]. [Discrimination of the Interest.
Reply to the remarks and Final reply to Anders Örne.]
(Tiden 23 (1931), pp. 591—599, 607—612.) [Cf. 19.]

13 * "Ekonomisk vetenskap och politisk ekonomi." Ett replik-
skifte mellan prof. G. Myrdal, Genève, och fil. d:r J. Åkerman, Stockholm. [Economic Science and Political Economy.
Exchange of replies . . .] (Statsvetenskaplig Tidskrift 34
(1931), pp. 429—446, [447—462], 463—473, [474—486].)

14 Kring den praktiska nationalekonomiens problematik. [On
Practical Political Economy and Its Complex of Problems.]
(Ekonomisk Tidskrift 33 (1931), pp. 41—81.)

15+ Om penningteoretisk jämvikt. En studie över den "normala
räntan" i Wicksells penninglära. [Monetary Equilibrium
from a Theoretical Point of View. A Study of the "Normal
Interest" According to Wicksell's ˉDoctrine of Money.]
(Ekonomisk Tidskrift 33 (1931), pp. 191—302.) [Cf. 91a.]

16 Penningkrisens upprinnelse. [The Origin of the Monetary
Crisis.] (Nordisk Tidskrift. Ny serie 7 (1931), pp. 517—534.)
[Cf. 19.]

17 Riktlinjer för svensk penningpolitik. [Guide Lines for the
Swedish Monetary Policy.] Stockholm 1931, pp. 13—25,

44—46. (Nationalekonomiska Föreningens Förhandlingar 1931, pp. 139—151, 170—172. [Off-print with special pagination.])

Lecture at a meeting of the Society of Political Economy (Stockholm), November 26, 1931.

18 Socialism eller kapitalism i framtidens Amerika? [Socialism or Capitalism in the United States of the Future.] (Tiden 23 (1931), pp. 205—230.)

19 Den svenska penningkrisen. [The Monetary Crisis in Sweden.] (Tiden 23 (1931), pp. 521—542.) [Cf. 16.]

Rejoinder by Anders Örne and the author's reply, New rejoinder by Örne and the author's final reply, see 12.

20+ Sveriges väg genom penningkrisen. Bilaga: Hur Sverige tvingades att överge guldmyntfoten. Av Karin Kock. [Sweden's Way out of the Monetary Crisis. Appendix: How Sweden Was Compelled to Leave the Gold Standard. By Karin Kock.] Stockholm, Natur och Kultur, 1931, 163 pp.

21 Valutabolsjevism. [Currency Bolshevism.] (Dagens Nyheter 22/12 1931.

1932

22 Folket och samhällsklasserna. [The People and the Classes of Society.] (Herlitz, Nils: Svensk samhällslära. Under medverkan av Gunnar Myrdal. 2:a uppl. Stockholm 1932, pp. 11—13.) [Cf. 6.]

23 Kosta sociala reformer pengar? [Do Social Reforms Cost Money?] (Arkitektur och samhälle. Stockholm 1932, pp. 33—44.)

2nd—3rd ed. same year.

24 Lantbrukets kris. [The Crisis of Agriculture.] (Svenskt Land 16 (1932): 2, pp. 30—31.)

25 Penningväsendet. [The Monetary System.] (Herlitz, Nils: Svensk samhällslära. Under medverkan av Gunnar Myrdal. 2:a uppl. Stockholm 1932, pp. 99—102.)

26 Das politische Element in der nationalökonomischen Doktrinbildung. [Orig. title: Vetenskap och politik i nationalekonomien.] Aus dem Schwedischen von Gerhard Mackenroth. Berlin, Junker & Dünnhaupt, 1932, XI, 309 pp. (Sozialwissenschaftliche Studien.) [Cf. 11c, 399.]

27 Samhällsrörelser och organisationer. [Social Movements and Organizations.] (Herlitz, Nils: Svensk samhällslära. Under medverkan av Gunnar Myrdal. 2:a uppl. Stockholm 1932, pp. 14—24.) [Cf. 7.]

28+ Socialpolitikens dilemma 1—2. [Dilemma of Social Welfare Policy.] (Spektrum 2 (1932): 3, pp. 1—13; 4, pp. 13—31.) [Cf. 29.]

29 Socialpolitikens Dilemma. [Dilemma of Social Welfare Policy.] (Socialt Tidsskrift 8 (1932): Afd. A, pp. 99—120.) [Cf. 28.]
Danish transl. of a lecture in the Society of Social Economy (Copenhagen), 20 January, 1932.

30 Staten och det ekonomiska livet. [The State and the Economic Life.] (Herlitz, Nils: Svensk samhällslära. Under medverkan av Gunnar Myrdal. 2:a uppl. Stockholm 1932, pp. 102—105.) [Cf. 9.]

31 Det svenska jordbrukets läge i världskrisen. [The Situation of Swedish Agriculture in the World Crisis. A lecture . . .] (Handlingar till Lantbruksveckan (Stockholm) 1932, pp. 21—41. [Off-print with special pagination 1—11.]) [Cf. 32.]
Lecture at the general meeting of the Agricultural Week (Stockholm), 14 March, 1932.

32 Det svenska jordbrukets läge i världskrisen. [The Situation of Swedish Agriculture in the World Crisis.] (Landtmannen 15 (1932): 12, pp. 243—246.)
Report of 31.

33 Sverige och krisen. [Sweden and the Crisis.] (Nationaløkonomisk Tidsskrift 70 (1932), pp. 1—21.)
Lecture in the Society of Political Economy (Copenhagen), 19 January, 1932.

34 Uppfinningars betydelse för den ekonomiska utvecklingen. [The Importance of Inventions for the Economic Development.] (Industritidningen Norden 1932, pp. 33—35.)
Lecture in the Swedish Inventors' Association, 15 December, 1931.

5

1933

35a+* Bostadsfrågan såsom socialt planläggningsproblem. Under krisen och på längre sikt. En undersökning rörande behovet av en utvidgning av bostadsstatistiken ... [With] Uno Åhrén. [The Housing Question as a Problem of Social Planning. During the Crisis and at Longer Sight. An Investigation of the Need of Extended Housing Statistics ...] Stockholm 1933, 111 pp. (SOU 1933: 14. Finansdepartementet.)

35b — Stockholm, Kooperativa Förbundet, 1933, 111 pp.

36+ * The Cost of Living in Sweden 1830—1930. By Gunnar Myrdal, assisted by Sven Bouvin. [Transl. from Swedish by E. Classen.] London, P. S. King & Son, 1933, XII, 251 pp. (Stockholm Economic Studies ... 2. — Wages, Cost of Living and National Income in Sweden 1860—1930 ... 1.)

38+ Der Gleichgewichtsbegriff als Instrument der geldtheoretischen Analyse. Aus dem Schwedischen übers. von Gerhard Mackenroth. (Beiträge zur Geldtheorie. Hrsg. von F. A. Hayek. Wien 1933, pp. 361—487.) [Cf. 91a.]

39 Industrialization and Population. (Economic Essays in Honour of Gustav Cassel. London 1933, pp. 435—457.)

40+ Konjunktur och offentlig hushållning. P. M. angående verkningarna på den ekonomiska konjunkturutvecklingen i Sverige av olika åtgärder inom den offentliga hushållningens område. [Business Cycles and Public Finance. Memorandum Concerning the Effects of Various Measures within the Public Sector on the Business Cycles in Sweden.] (Bihang till riksdagens protokoll 1933. Saml. 1. Bilaga 3. Stockholm 1933, 46 pp.) [Cf. 41.]

41 Konjunktur och offentlig hushållning. En utredning. [Business Cycles and Public Finance. An Investigation.] Stockholm, Kooperativa Förbundet, 1933, 76 pp. (Ekonomiska debatten 2.) [Off-print of 40, slightly rev.]

42+ Das Zweck-Mittel-Denken in der Nationalökonomie. [Übers. aus dem Schwedischen Manuskript von Gerhard Mackenroth.] (Zeitschrift für Nationalökonomie 4: 3. 1933, pp. 305 —329.) [Cf. 279².]

1934

43 * Bostaden och vår ekonomi. [Medarbetare: ... Gunnar Myrdal ...] [The Housing and Our Economy. Contributors: ...] Stockholm, Hyresgästernas Förlag, 1934, 87 pp.

44a+ Finanspolitikens ekonomiska verkningar. [The Economic Effects of Fiscal Policy.] Stockholm 1934, XII, 279 pp. (Arbetslöshetsutredningens betänkande 2. Bilagor 2. — SOU 1934: 1. Socialdepartementet.)

44b Translation.
[Spanish:] Los efectos económicos de la política fiscal. Madrid 1948. (194)

45a+* Kris i befolkningsfrågan. [The Population Problem in Crisis.] [With] Alva Myrdal. Stockholm, Bonnier, 1934, 332 pp. [Cf. 55.]
2nd ed. same year.

45b — Folkuppl. [= 3:e omarb. och utv. uppl.] [Popular ed. = 3rd rev. and enl. ed. ...] Stockholm 1935. (55)

45c Translations.
[Danish:] Krise i Befolknings-Spørgsmaalet. København 1935. (56)
[Norwegian:] Krisen i befolkningsspørsmålet. Oslo 1936. (67)

46 Det penningpolitiska läget. [The Monetary Situation.] (Internationella ekonomiska frågor. Stockholm 1934, pp. 185—197.)

_____

47 * Avfolkning eller samhällsreform. [Depopulation or Social Reform.] [With] Alva Myrdal. (Svenska Dagbladet 6/12 1934.)

1935

48 Det aktuella befolkningspolitiska läget. Ett uttalande. [The Present Situation of the Population Policy. A Statement.] (Frisinnad Ungdom 1, 1935, p. 1.)

49 Befolkningsfrågan och kvinnofrågan. [Population Question and Women's Movement.] (Hertha 22 (1935), pp. 81—83.)

50 Befolkningsproblemet i Sverige. En studieorientering. [The Population Problem in Sweden. Orientation of Studies.] Stockholm, ABF, 1935, 20 pp. (Arbetarnas Bildningsförbunds Centralbyrå.)
Broadcast lecture, 27 January, 1935.

51 * Betänkande med förslag rörande lån och årliga bidrag av statsmedel för främjande av bostadsförsörjning för mindre bemedlade barnrika familjer jämte därtill hörande utredningar. Avgivet den 17 januari av bostadssociala utredningen. [Report with Proposal regarding Subsidies and Annual Contributions from the Government in order to Promote the Supplying with Housing Accommodation to large Families in Poor Circumstances.] [By Gunnar Myrdal and others.] Stockholm 1935, 1*—86*, 1—265 pp. (SOU 1935: 2. Socialdepartementet.)

52 Debatt i befolkningsfrågan. Inledningsanförande. — Avslutningsanförande. [Debate on the Population Problem. Introductory Speech. — Concluding Remarks.] Stockholm 1935, pp. 6—22, 71—79.
Broadcast discussion, 9 April, 1935.

53+ Den förändrade världsbilden inom nationalekonomin. [The Altered World Image in Political Economy.] (Samhällskrisen och socialvetenskaperna. Två installationsföreläsningar. Stockholm, Kooperativa Förbundet, 1935, pp. 5, 7—41.)
Inaugural lecture at Stockholm University, 31 March, 1935. — Printed together with Tingsten, Herbert: Statskunskapen och den politiska utvecklingen. — Preface written jointly by both authors.

54 Jordbrukspolitik — planmässig och på längre sikt. [Agricultural Policy — Planned and with a Far-Away Aim.] (Konsumentbladet 22 (1935): 31, pp. 3, 14; 33, pp. 6, 14.)

55 * Kris i befolkningsfrågan. [The Population Problem in Crisis.] [With] Alva Myrdal. Folkuppl. [= 3:e omarb. och utv. uppl.] [Popular ed. = 3rd rev. and enl. ed.] Stockholm, Bonnier, 1935, 403 pp. [Cf. 45a—c.]
4th—7th ed. same year.

56 * Krise i Befolknings-Spørgsmaalet. [The Population Problem in Crisis.] [With] Alva Myrdal. Autoriseret dansk Udg. ved [Authorized Danish ed. by] Jørgen S. Dich. (Udg. af Dansk Forening for social Oplysning, Det sociale Sekretariat, ved Udv. for social Litteratur.) København, Martin, 1935, 320 pp. (Nyt Socialt Bibliotek.) [Cf. 45c.]

57 Krise i befolkningsspørsmålet. [The Population Problem in Crisis.] (Fritt Ord 1935, pp. 105—130.)
Principal substance of two conferences in the local branches in Bergen and Trondheim of the Norden Society.

58 Om studiet av befolkningsfrågan. [On the Study of the Population Problem.] (Studiebrev nr 1 i serien "Befolkningsfrågan". [Stockholm] 1935, pp. 1—2.) [Cf. 59.]
Extract from an address to leaders of groups of listeners.

59 * Studiebrev i serien "Befolkningsfrågan". [Study Letters in the Series "The Population Problem".] 1—11. (Stockholm], Radiotjänst, 1935—36, 1—4 pp. per brev.) [Cf. 58.]
The letters are elaborated in consultation with the conductor of the course, Gunnar Myrdal.

60 * Vårt folks framtid. Uttalanden i befolkningsfrågan vid kyrkliga mötet i Stockholm 1935 av Karl Arvid Edin, Rut Grubb, Gunnar Myrdal, Arvid Runestam. [Our People's Future. Contributions to the Population Issue at the Church Meeting in Stockholm 1935 by . . .] Stockholm, Fritze, 1935, 69 pp. [Myrdal pp. 28—54.]

1936

61 Aktuella beskattningsproblem. [Present Problems of Taxation.] (Nationalekonomiska Föreningens Förhandlingar 1936, pp. 91—115 [incl. discussion].)
Lecture at a meeting of the Society of Political Economy (Stockholm), November 12, 1936.

62 Allmänna och ekonomiska synpunkter på befolkningsutvecklingen. [General and Economic Aspects on the Development of Population.] (Nordisk Försäkringstidskrift 1936, pp. 199—212.)
Shorthand account of an address at the meeting of the Swedish Insurance Association, January 31, 1936.

63   * Betänkande angående dels planmässigt sparande och dels statliga bosättningslån. Avgivet av befolkningskommissionen. [Report on Methodical Saving and Public Housing Credits Delivered by the Population Commission.] [Mainly written by Gunnar Myrdal.] Stockholm 1936, 55 pp. (SOU 1936: 14. Socialdepartementet.)

64   * Betänkande angående familjebeskattning. Avgivet av befolkningskommissionen. [Report concerning Family Taxation. Delivered by the Population Commission.] [Mainly written by Gunnar Myrdal.] Stockholm 1936, 147 pp. (SOU 1936: 13. Finansdepartementet.)

65⁺ * Betänkande i sexualfrågan. Avgivet av befolkningskommissionen. [Report on the Sexual Question. Delivered by the Population Commission.] [Mainly written by Gunnar Myrdal.] Stockholm 1936, 452 pp. (SOU 1936: 59. Socialdepartementet.)

66   Familjesynpunkten på bostaden. [Family View on the Dwelling-Place.] (Andra allmänna svenska bostadskongressen. Stockholm den 29—30 nov. 1935. Föredrag . . . Stockholm 1936, pp. 22—80 [incl. discussion].)

67   * Krisen i befolkningsspørsmålet. [The Population Problem in Crisis.] [Orig. title:] Kris i befolkningsfrågan. [With] Alva Myrdal. Norsk utg. ved [Norwegian ed. by] Aase Lionæs og Arne Skaug. Oslo, Tiden, 1936, 404 pp. [Cf. 45c.]

68⁺ Några metodiska anmärkningar rörande befolkningsfrågans innebörd och vetenskapliga behandling. [Some Methodological Notes on the Population Problem and Its Scientific Treatment.] (Betänkande i sexualfrågan. Avgivet av befolkningskommissionen. Bilaga 1 = SOU 1936: 59. Socialdepartementet, pp. 149—158.) [Cf. 83.]

69   * Utsikterna i fråga om den framtida befolkningsutvecklingen i Sverige och de ekonomiska verkningarna av olika alternativt möjliga befolkningsutvecklingar. [The Prospects in regard to the Future Population Development in Sweden and the Economic Effects of Alternatively Possible Popula-

tion Developments.] [With] Sven Wicksell. Stockholm 1936, [43 pp.]. (SOU 1936: 59. Socialdepartementet. Bilaga 8, pp. 252—295.) [Cf. 87.]

70 Vad gäller striden i befolkningsfrågan? [What Is the Struggle in the Population Problem All About?] Stockholm, Frihet, 1936, 36 pp.

71 Vår lösen är: Hemmet, familjen. Vi förtröttas icke förrän vi segrat. [Our Watchword Is: Our Home, Our Family. We Won't Give up until We Have Won.] (Hus och Härd 1936: september, pp. 3, 8.)

Address at Skansen (Stockholm) at a meeting of Tenants' Association, Augusti 23, 1936.

72 Våra sociala syftlinjer. [Our Social Aims.] (Frihet 20 (1936): 17, pp. 3—4.)

73 * Yttrande angående revision av 18 kap. 13 § strafflagen m. m. Avgivet av befolkningskommissionen. [Statement concerning Revision of Chap. 18, § 13 of the Penal Law, etc. Delivered by the Population Commission. By Gunnar Myrdal and others.] Stockholm 1936, pp. 1—55. Bilagor pp. 1*—54*. (SOU 1936: 51. Socialdepartementet.)

---

74 Högerns socialpolitiska intresse. [The Conservative Party and Its Interest in Social Policy.] (Länstidningen (Östersund) 12/9 1936. — Skaraborgaren 14/9 1936. — Piteå-Tidningen 16/9 1936. — Ny Tid 17/9 1936. — Skånska Social-Demokraten 18/9 1936, etc.)

1937

76 Massfattigdomen och dess avskaffande. [Mass Poverty and Its Abolition.] (Frihet 21 (1937): 9, pp. 4—5.)

77+ Den svenska penningpolitiken inför faran av en fortsatt pris-stegring. [The Swedish Monetary Policy and the Menace of a Further Rise in Prices.] (SAP Information 1937: pp. 161—167, 177—187.)

---

78 [Foreword to:] Hasselquist, Nils: Jordmonopolet en vidunder-
lig orättvisa. [Land Monopoly — a Monstrous Injustice.]
Stockholm 1937, pp. 3—4.

1938

79 * Betänkande i näringsfrågan. Avgivet av befolkningskommissionen. [Report Concerning the Food Problem. Delivered
by the Population Commission.] [Mainly written by Gunnar
Myrdal.] Stockholm 1938, 173 pp. [Bilagor] pp. 1*—251*.
(SOU 1938: 6. Socialdepartementet.) [Cf. 84.]

80+ Jordbrukspolitiken under omläggning. [The Evolution of
Agricultural Policy.] [P. 1—2.] Stockholm, Kooperativa
Förbundet, 1938, 126 pp.
P. 2 = Översiktlig analys av det jordbrukspolitiska problemet i Sverige
på något längre sikt. (84)

81 Jordbrukspolitikens svårigheter. [The Problems of the Agricultural Policy.] (Nationalekonomiska Föreningens Förhandlingar 1938, pp. 57—98 [incl. discussion].)
Lecture at the meeting of the Society of Political Economy (Stockholm),
March 3, 1938.

82+ Kontant eller in natura i socialpolitiken. [Payment in Cash
or in Kind in Social Policy.] (Nationaløkonomisk Tidsskrift 76 (1938), pp. 69—91.)
Lecture in the Society of Political Economy (Copenhagen), January 25,
1938.

83 Några metodiska anmärkningar rörande befolkningsfrågans
innebörd och vetenskapliga behandling . . . [Some Methodological Notes on the Population Problem and Its Scientific
Treatment.] (Betänkande i sexualfrågan. Avgivet av befolkningskommissionen. Bilaga 1 = SOU 1936: 59. Socialdepartementet. 2:a uppl. Stockholm 1938, pp. 149—158.) [Cf. 68.]

84 Översiktlig analys av det jordbrukspolitiska problemet i
Sverige på något längre sikt. [Analysis of the Problem of
Agricultural Policy in Sweden at a Somewhat Longer Sight.]
(Betänkande i näringsfrågan. Avgivet av befolkningskom-
missionen. Stockholm 1938. Bilaga 2, pp. 74*—92*. =
SOU 1938: 6. Socialdepartementet.) [Cf. 79.]
P. 2 of Jordbrukspolitiken under omläggning. (80)

85 Socialpolitik in natura. [Social Policy in Kind.] (Första Maj 1938, pp. 31—32.)

86 * [That Wonderful Swedish Budget. By the editors of Fortune, in consultation with Professor Gunnar Myrdal.] (Fortune 18: 3 (September 1938), pp. 65—66, 130, 134, 136, 138, 140, 142, 145.)

87 * Utsikterna i fråga om den framtida befolkningsutvecklingen i Sverige . . . [The Prospects in regard to the Future Population Development in Sweden . . .] [With] Sven Wicksell. 2:a uppl. [2nd ed.] Stockholm 1938, [43 pp.]. (SOU 1936: 59. Bilaga 8, pp. 252—295.) [Identical with 1st ed. (69)]

---

88 Befolkningspolitiken i Sverige blir aktuell på allvar först om tio år. [The Population Policy in Sweden Will Be of Current Interest Only in Ten Years.] (Social-Demokraten 12/8 1938.) Interview.

1939

89+ Fiscal Policy in the Business Cycle. (The American Economic Review 29 (1939): 1. P. 2. Suppl., pp. 183—193.)

90 Maintaining Democracy in Sweden. Two articles. 1. With Dictators as Neighbors. — 2. The Defenses of Democracy. Second of two articles on the Swedish Way. New York, Albert Bonnier, [1939], 14 pp. [Cf. 93.]
Repr. from Survey Graphic 28 (1939), pp. 309—311, 351—352, 354—355, 357.

91a+Monetary Equilibrium. London . . ., Hodge, 1939, XI, 214 pp.
The original Swedish text, "Om penningteoretisk jämvikt" (15) . . . was a condensation of a series of lectures on Wicksell's monetary theory . . . A German translation entitled „Der Gleichgewichtsbegriff als Instrument der geldtheoretischen Analyse" was included in the Beiträge zur Geldtheorie . . . Wien 1933. (38) . . . As now published in English, the essay is a rev. adaptation of the German text. Transl. by B. B. Bryce and N. Stolper.

91b — New York 1962. (365)

91c — London 1963. (397)

91d — New York 1965. (469)

91e Translations.
[French:] L'équilibre monétaire. Paris 1950. (208)
[Italian. Cf. 1050.]
[Japanese:] Kaheiteki kinkoron. Tōkyō 1943. (113)

92 * Taxation and Recovery. [By Alfred G. Buehler . . . Gunnar
Myrdal . . .] (The 2nd Fortune Round Table 1939, (VI),
33 pp.)
Repr. from Fortune for May, 1939, pp. 67—68, 110, 113—114, 116—118,
120, 123—124, 126.

93 With Dictators as Neighbors. (Survey Graphic 28 (1939),
pp. 309—311, 351—352, 354—355, 357.) [Cf. 90.]
Adapted from the author's Bronson Cutting Memorial Lecture in Washington in spring, 1939.

1940

94a+Population. A Problem for Democracy. Cambridge, Mass.,
Harvard University Press, 1940, XIII, 238 pp.
The Godkin Lectures, 1938. — Repr. 1962.

94b — Magnolia, Mass., 1969. (717)

94c Translation.
[Japanese:] Jinko mondai to shakai seisaku. Tōkyō 1943. (112)

95 Vad får vi veta och vad är sant i nyheterna från utlandet?
[What Do We Get to Know and What Is True of the News
from Abroad?] (Vi 27 (1940): 47, pp. 3, 14.)

96 "Vi får inte vara likgiltiga för vad som händer i världen
omkring oss." [We Mustn't Be Indifferent to What Happens
Around Us in the World.] (Vi 27 (1940): 51/52, p. 12.)
Contribution to a table talk in Stockholm, 2 December, 1940, about
Swedish independent Government.

1941

97 * Återseende med den svenska pressen. [Meeting Again with the Swedish Press.] (Publicistklubbens Årsbok 1941, pp. 83—86.)
Extract of a lecture [with Alva Myrdal] in the Press Club (Stockholm), November 9, 1940.

98a⁺* Kontakt med Amerika. [Contact with America.] [With] Alva Myrdal. Stockholm, Bonnier, & Helsingfors, Söderström, 1941, 373 pp. [Cf. 149.]

98b Translations.
[Danish:] Kontakt med Amerika. København 1946. (174)
[Dutch:] Contact met Amerika. Den Haag 1948. (193)
[German:] Kontakt mit Amerika. Stockholm 1944. (138)

99⁺ Samtal mellan svensk och tysk. [A Dispute between a Swede and a German.] (Vi 28 (1941): 5, pp. 3, 14.)

1942

100 Den amerikanska världsbilden. [= Amerika i världskriget och i världsfreden 2.] [The American World Image ...] (Vi 29 (1942): 50, pp. 9—10.) [Cf. 106.]

101 Amerikas ställning till bundsförvanter och fiender. [= Amerika i världskriget och i världsfreden 3.] [America's Position to Allies and Enemies ...] (Vi 29 (1942): 51/52, pp. 3—4.) [Cf. 108.]

102 Keizai-gakusetsu to seijiteki yōso. [Japanese transl. of Das politische Element in der nationalökonomischen Doktrinbildung.] [Transl. by:] Yuzo Yamada. Tōkyō, Nihon Hyoron Sha, [1942], (22), 412, 29, (14) pp. [Cf. 26, 570.]

103 Pearl Harbour som vändpunkt. [= Amerika i världskriget och i världsfreden 1.] [Pearl Harbour as a Turning-Point ...] (Vi 29 (1942): 47, pp. 3—4.) [Cf. 120.]

1943

104⁺ Amerika mitt i världen. [America in the Center of the World.] Stockholm, Kooperativa Förbundet, 1943, 128 pp.
Contents: Pearl Harbor som vändpunkt. (103) — Den amerikanska

världsbilden. (106) — Amerikas ställning till bundsförvanter och fiender. (108) — Amerika och Norden. (105) — Återverkningar inom Amerika av dess nya ställning i världen. (109) — Negerfrågan i Amerika just nu. (116) — Rasfrågan i världspolitiken. (122) — Konjunkturpolitik och social välfärdspolitik. (114) — Monopolism och industriell expansion. (115) — Det internationella återuppbyggnadsproblemet. (136)

The articles, except the last one, were printed in Vi 1942—1943 but are revised and considerably amended.

105 Amerika och Norden. [= Amerika i världskriget och i världsfreden 4.] [America and the Northern Countries . . .] (Vi 30 (1943): 2, pp. 3—4, 22. — 104: Amerika mitt i världen, pp. 38—52.)

106 Den amerikanska världsbilden. [= Amerika i världskriget och i världsfreden 2.] [The American World Image . . .] (104: Amerika mitt i världen, pp. 17—24.)

107 Amerikas kultur omgestaltas. [= Amerika i världskriget och i världsfreden 5.] [The American Culture Is Being Transformed . . .] (Vi 30 (1943): 3, pp. 3—4.)
Also published with the title: Återverkningar inom Amerika av dess nya ställning i världen. (104, 109)

108 Amerikas ställning till bundsförvanter och fiender. [= Amerika i världskriget och i världsfreden 3.] [America's Position to Allies and Enemies . . .] (104: Amerika mitt i världen, pp. 25—37.) [Cf. 101.]

109 Återverkningar inom Amerika av dess nya ställning i världen. [Reactions within America of Its New Position in the World.] (104: Amerika mitt i världen, pp. 53—60.)
Also published with the title: Amerikas kultur omgestaltas. (107)

110 Ekonomi och välfärdspolitik i Amerika. [= Amerika i världskriget och i världsfreden 8.] [Economy and Welfare Policy in America . . .] (Vi 30 (1943): 7, pp. 9—10.)
Also published with the title: Konjunkturpolitik och social välfärdspolitik. (114)

111 L'elemento politico nella formazione delle dottrine dell'economia pura. [Orig. title: Vetenskap och politik i nationalekonomien. Transl. of the German ed.: Das politische Element in der nationalökonomischen Doktrinbildung.] Firenze,

G. C. Sansoni, 1943, 341 pp. (Biblioteca Sansoni di economia 1.) [Cf. 11c, 26.]

112 Jinko mondai to shakai seisaku. [Japanese transl. of: Population. A Problem for Democracy.] [Transl. by:] Kazuhiko Kawakazu. Tōkyō, Kyowa Shobo, 1943, 202 pp. [Cf. 94c.]

113 Kaheiteki kinkoron. [Japanese transl. of: Monetary Equilibrium.] [Transl. by:] Shozo Sobashima. Tōkyō, Jitsugyo no Nihon Sha, 1943, 258 pp. [Cf. 91c.]

114 Konjunkturpolitik och social välfärdspolitik. [Fluctuations of Economic Policy and Welfare Policy in America ...] (104: Amerika mitt i världen, pp. 82—91.)
Also published with the title: Ekonomi och välfärdspolitik i Amerika. (110).

115 Monopolism och industriell expansion. [= Amerika i världskriget och i världsfreden 9.] [Monopolism and Industrial Expansion ...] (Vi 30 (1943): 9, pp. 7—8, 15. — 104: Amerika mitt i världen, pp. 92—104.)

116 Negerfrågan i Amerika just nu. [= Amerika i världskriget och i världsfreden 6.] [The Negro Problem in America Right Now ...] (Vi 30 (1943): 4, pp. 3—4, 18. — 104: Amerika mitt i världen, pp. 61—71.)

117 Negro and America's Uneasy Conscience. (Free World 6 (1943): November, pp. 412—422.)

118 Nordiskt samarbete i fredskrisen. [Northern Cooperation in the Peace Crisis.] (Nordens Tidning 1 (1943): 2, pp. 13—14.) [Cf. 136.]
Summary of a lecture at the meeting of the Society of Political Economy (Stockholm), 5 March, 1943.

119 Not om engångsskatt på förmögenhet. [Note on the Capital Levy Problem.] (Ekonomisk Tidskrift 45 (1943), pp. 47—57.)

120 Pearl Harbor som vändpunkt. [= Amerika i världskriget och i världsfreden 1.] [Pearl Harbor as a Turning-Point ...] (104: Amerika mitt i världen, pp. 7—16.) [Cf. 103.]

121 Rasfrågan i världskriget. [= Amerika i världskriget och i världsfreden 7.] [The Racial Question in the World War ...] (Vi 30 (1943): 5, pp. 9—11.) [Identical with 122.]

122 Rasfrågan i världspolitiken. [The Racial Question in the World Politics.] (104: Amerika mitt i världen, pp. 72—81.) [Identical with 121.]

123 Tillbaka till internationalismen. ⌊Back to the Internationalism.] (Första Maj 1943, pp. 10—11.)

124 Willkie och världen. [Willkie and the World.] (Vi 30 (1943): 30, pp. 12—13.)
Review of Willkie, W. L.: One World. London 1943; Swedish transl.: En värld. Stockholm 1943.

———

125 Efterkrigstidens ekonomi. [Post-War Economy.] (Aftontidningen 1943: 29/3.)
Review of Lewis L. Lorwin: Det andra världskrigets ekonomiska följder [Economic Consequences of the 2nd World War], New York 1941.

126 Gunnar heter jag. [My Name Is Gunnar.] (Aftontidningen 16/8 1943.)
Brief autobiography with the rubric: Svenskar i täten. Femtionde porträttet. Gunnar Myrdal. En positiv radikal.

1944

127a⁺An American Dilemma. The Negro Problem and Modern Democracy. With the assistance of Richard Sterner and Arnold Rose. Vol. 1—2. New York & London, Harper, 1944, pp. I—LV, 1—706; I—XII, 707—1483. [Also ed. in one vol.] [Cf. 128, 199, 276, 279¹, 280—281, 285, 289, 298, 354, 361, 426, 474, 557, 636, 659, 710, 744, 758, 763, 783, 793, 795, 807—808, 845—846, 853, 870, 881, 892, 898—899, 969.]
Appendices: 1. A Methodological Note on Valuations and Beliefs. (141, — 2. A Methodological Note on Facts and Valuations in Social Science. (139) — 3. A Methodological Note on the Principle of Cumulation. [Also with the title:] The Principle of Cumulation. (140, 289, 426, 473, 511) ... — 5. A Parallel to the Negro Problem. (142, 812,

1033) — 6. Pre-War Conditions of the Negro Wage Earner . . . (143)
— 7. Distribution of Negro Residences in Selected Cities. (129) —
8. Research on Caste and Class in Negro Community. (145) —
9. Researches in Negro Leadership. (146) — 10. Quantitative Studies
of Race Attitudes. (144)

9 issues same year.

127b — New York & Evanston 1962. (355)

127c — New York, Toronto & London 1964. (410)

127d — New York, Evanston & London 1969. (697)

127e — New York [& Toronto 1975]. (1015^3)

128   America's Present and Future Economy. (The XXth
      Century 7 (1944), pp. 239—247.)
      A condensed adaptation of the author's chapters in An American Dilemma
      [= Part IV]. [Cf. 127a.]

129   Distribution of Negro Residences in Selected Cities. (127a:
      An American Dilemma . . . Appendix 7. Vol. 2, pp. 1125—
      1128.)

130⁺ Den ekonomiska utvecklingen i Amerika och konjunkturut-
      sikterna. [The Economic Growth in America and the
      Business Cycles Prospects.] (Nationalekonomiska Föreningens
      Förhandlingar 1944, pp. 31—53.) [Cf. 137.]
      Address to the meeting of the Society of Political Economy (Stockholm),
      9 March, 1944.

131   Front mot efterkrigsdepression. [Preventing Post-War
      Depression.] (Vår Väg 1944: 4, p. 3.)

132   Handels- och valutapolitik. [Commerce and Monetary
      Policy.] (Mellanfolkligt Samarbete 14 (1944): 7/8, pp. 160—
      162.)
      Report of an address in Stockholm, October 14, 1944.

133⁺ Höga skatter och låga räntor. [High Taxes, Low Interests.]
      (Studier i ekonomi och historia. Tillägnade Eli F. Heckscher.
      Uppsala 1944, pp. 160—169.)

The main thoughts of this paper were presented for the first time in a lecture in the Club of Political Economy of the Federal Reserve Board, Washington, D. C., in November, 1943.

134 Inflation eller socialism. [Inflation or Socialism.] (Fackföreningsrörelsen 24 (1944): 2, pp. 318—322.)
Lecture to a Trade Union Meeting in Stockholm.

135 De internationella förhandlingarna i Washington om ekonomiska efterkrigsproblem. [The International Discussions in Washington on Post-War Problems.] (Skrifter utg. av Svenska Bankföreningen 75. Stockholm 1944, 36 pp.)
Address to the Swedish Bankers' Association, 29 March, 1944.

136 Det internationella återuppbyggnadsproblemet. [The International Problem of Reconstruction.] (Nationalekonomiska Föreningens Förhandlingar 1943 [pr. 1944], pp. 35—56 [incl. discussion]. — 104: Amerika mitt i världen, pp. 105—128.) [Cf. 118.]
Lecture at a meeting of the Society of Political Economy (Stockholm), 5 March, 1943.

137 Is American Business Deluding Itself? (The Atlantic, November 1944, pp. 51—58.)
Address based upon Den ekonomiska utvecklingen i Amerika och konjunkturutsikterna. (130)

138 * Kontakt mit Amerika. [Orig. titles: Kontakt med Amerika — Amerika mitt i världen.] [With] Alva Myrdal. Aus dem Schwedischen übertr. und bearb. von Walter A. Berendsohn. Stockholm, Bermann-Fischer, 1944, 253 pp. (Bücher zur Weltpolitik [1].) [Cf. 98b, 104.]

139 A Methodological Note on Facts and Valuations in Social Science. (127a: An American Dilemma ... Appendix 2. Vol. 2, pp. 1035—1064.)

140 A Methodological Note on the Principle of Cumulation. (127a: An American Dilemma ... Appendix 3. Vol. 2, pp. 1065—1070.) [Identical with 289. Cf. 511.]

141 A Methodological Note on Valuations and Beliefs. (127a: An American Dilemma . . . Appendix 1. Vol. 2, pp. 1027—1034.) [Cf. 659.]

142 A Parallel to the Negro Problem. (127a: An American Dilemma . . . Appendix 5. Vol. 2, pp. 1073—1078.) [Cf. 812.]

143 Pre-War Conditions of the Negro Wage Earner in Selected Industries and Occupations. (127a: An American Dilemma . . . Appendix 6. Vol. 2, pp. 1079—1124.)

144 Quantitative Studies of Race Attitudes. (127a: An American Dilemma . . . Appendix 10. Vol. 2, pp. 1136—1143.)

145 Research on Caste and Class in Negro Community. (127a: An American Dilemma . . . Appendix 8. Vol. 2, pp. 1129—1132.)

146 Researches in Negro Leadership. (127a: An American Dilemma . . . Appendix 9. Vol. 2, pp. 1133—1135.)

147 Samhällsvetenskapernas utbyggnad vid universiteten och de fria högskolorna. [The Future of Social Sciences at Swedish Universities.] (Ekonomisk Tidskrift 46 (1944), pp. 245—272.)
Lecture on October 1, 1944, at the meeting of the Society of Social Sciences (Stockholm).

148 Sveriges ekonomiska efterkrigsproblem. [Sweden's Economic Post-War Problems.] (Svenskt Affärsliv 12 (1944), pp. 160—164.)
Address at the annual meeting of the Swedish Wholesalers' Association, 11 May, 1944.

149 * Sweden's Profile in America. [With] Alva Myrdal. (American Swedish Historical Museum. Yearbook 1944, pp. 1—27.)
Authorized transl. of chapter 10 of the author's Kontakt med Amerika. (98a)

150a⁺ Varning för fredsoptimism. [Warning for Post-War Optimism.] Stockholm, Bonnier, 1944, 355 pp. [Cf. 151.]

150b Translation.
[German:] Warnung vor Friedensoptimismus. Zürich & New York 1945. (165)

151 Varning för fredsoptimism! [Warning for Post-War Optimism!] (Karlstads Stiftsblad 24 (1944), pp. 187—188.) Extract from: Varning för fredsoptimism, pp. 302—308. (150)

_____

152 [Foreword to:] Franklin, Jay, [pseud. for Carter, John Franklin]: Amerika göres om ... [Orig. title: Remaking America.] Stockholm 1944, pp. 5—7. The original published in 1942.

153 Den ekonomiska efterkrigsplaneringen. [The Post-War Economic Planning.] 1—2. (Morgon-Tidningen 25/8, 26/8 1944.)

154 Staten och köpkraften. [The State and the Purchasing Power.] 1—2. (Morgon-Tidningen 2/11, 4/11 1944.) Address at an information meeting of the Stockholm Merchants' Association.

1945

155+ Gustav Cassel in memoriam. (Ekonomisk Revy 2 (1945), pp. 3—13.) [Cf. 226, 394, 464, 826.]

156 Den juridiska vetenskapens ställning och de juridiska studiernas anordning i Sverige. [The Position of Jurisprudence and the Organization of Legal Studies in Sweden.] (Svensk Juristtidning 30 (1945), pp. 357—363.)

157 Neutraliteten och vårt samvete. [Neutrality and Our Conscience.] (Tiden 37 (1945), pp. 257—270.)

158 Planhushållningsdebatten. [The Debate on Planned Economy.] (Tiden 37 (1945), pp. 517—521.) Reply to Gerard De Geer: En företagares syn på socialisering och planhushållning. [An Employer's View of Socialization and Planned Economy.] (Tiden 37 (1945), pp. 464—469.)

159+ Relation to Specialized Agencies in the Economic and Social Field. (Peace and Security after the Second World War. A Swedish Contribution to the Subject. Published by the Swedish Institute of International Affairs. [Stockholm] 1945, pp. 173—191.) [Cf. 161.]

160 Socialiseringsdebatten i Borgarskolan [den 24 maj 1945]. [The Socialization Debate in the "Burghers' School".] (Industria 41 (1945), pp. 656—662. [Off-print with special pagination 1—7.])

161 Speciella organ på det ekonomiska och sociala området. [Specialized Agencies in the Economic and Social Field.] (Fred och säkerhet efter andra världskriget. Uppsala 1945, pp. 162—181.) [Cf. 159.]

162 Tiden och partiet. [Tiden and the Party.] (Tiden 37 (1945): pp. 1—9.) [Cf. 296.]

163+ Universitetsreform. [University Reform.] Stockholm, Tiden, 1945, 84 pp.

164 Utrikespolitisk enighet. [Unity in Foreign Politics.] (Tiden 37 (1945), pp. 129—137.)

165 Warnung vor Friedensoptimismus. Schwedische Original-ausg.: Varning för fredsoptimism. [Übertr. von Verner Arpe.] Zürich & New York, Europa-Verlag, 1945, 240 pp. (Neue internationale Bibliothek 1.) [Cf. 150.]

---

166 Ekonomiskt samarbete inom Norden. [Economic Coopera-tion in the Northern Countries.] (Morgon-Tidningen 18/12 1945.)
Section of a discourse of the Minister of Trade [G. Myrdal] in the Association of Commerce in Gothenburg, Dec. 18, 1945.

167 'Food Stamps' for Furniture Planned for Sweden's Future. (Minneapolis Sunday Tribune 1945: October 14.)

23

168 Genom diskussion till klarhet. [Through Discussion to Clarity.] (Svenska Dagbladet 10/3 1945.)
Polemics with Allan Hernelius.

169 Socialdemokratin och frihandeln. [Social Democrats and Free Trade.] (Morgon-Tidningen 15/12 1945.)
Section of a discourse of the Minister of Trade [G. Myrdal] in the Chamber of Commerce in Stockholm, Dec. 14, 1945.

170 Staten och industrin. [State and Industry.] (Morgon-Tidningen 30/11, 1/12 1945.) [Not identical with 177.]
Shortened ed. of the author's contribution to a broadcast discussion.

171 Utbildning nu — kan rädda från kris. [Education today — Can Save us from a Crisis.] (På fritid 1945: 2, p. 2.)
Interview.

1946

172 All debatt är av godo. [Any Kind of Debate Is Profitable.] (Vi 33 (1946): 6, pp. 11—12.)

173 Fri handel och full sysselsättning. [Free Trade and Full Employment.] (Vi 33 (1946): 1, pp. 3—4, 26—27.)

174 * Kontakt med Amerika. [With] Alva Myrdal. [Sammendrag og Overs. af Kontakt med Amerika, Varning för fredsoptimism, Amerika mitt i världen ved Ulf Ekman.] [Contact with America. Summary and transl. ...] København, Athenæum, 1946, 320 pp. [Cf. 98b, 104, 150.]

175 The Reconstruction of World Trade and Swedish Trade Policy. (Suppl. B to Svenska Handelsbankens Index, December 1946, pp. 3—30.) [Cf. 179, 182.]
Transl. of a paper read before the Society of Political Economy (Stockholm), December 5, 1946.

177 Staten och industrin. [State and Industry.] (Industria 42 (1946): 3, pp. 41—50. [Off-print 1946, 8 pp.]) [Not identical with 170.]
Lecture in the Stockholm Merchants' Association, January 8, 1946.

178 Svensk frihandelspolitik. [Swedish Free Commercial Policy.] (Svensk Utrikeshandel 1946: 12, pp. 9—12. [Off-print 1946, 14 pp.])

A summary of the principal arguments of a broadcast lecture in Norway, June 3, 1946.

179 Svenska handelspolitiken efter kriget. [The Swedish Commercial Policy after the War.] (Fackföreningsrörelsen 1946: 2, pp. 579—589.) [Cf. 175, 182.]

P. 1 of a lecture, December 5, 1946, in the Society of Political Economy (Stockholm).

180 Sweden Actively Furthering Free Foreign Trade. (The Commercial and Financial Chronicle, July 25, 1946, pp. 477, 504—505. [Off-print 1946, 7 pp.])

181 Våra handelsförbindelser. [Our Commercial Relations.] (Första Maj 1946, pp. 4—5.)

182 Världshandelns återuppbyggnad. [The Reconstruction of World Trade.] (Svensk Utrikeshandel 1946: 26, pp. 7—11.) [Cf. 175, 179.]

P. 2 of a lecture, December 5, 1946, in the Society of Political Economy (Stockholm).

---

183 Fisken i vår handelspolitik. [The Role of Fish in Our Commercial Policy.] (Morgon-Tidningen 24/5 1946.)

184 Socialdemokratisk Fremtidsprogram. [Social Democratic Programme for the Future.] 1—2. (Social-Demokraten [Copenhagen] 28/2, 1/3 1946.)

Address to the Workmen's Reading Association (Copenhagen).

185 [Intervju med Gunnar Myrdal angående det planerade svensk-ryska handelsavtalet.] [Interview . . . concerning the Planned Swedish-Russian Trade Agreement.] (Svenska Dagbladet 20/9 1946.)

Swedish transl. of an interview in The New York Herald Tribune 19/9 1946. — Interview by Wilfrid Fleisher.

186 Jag trivs bland företagarna. Min politik är inte fientlig . . . [I Feel at Home Among Employers. My Policy Is Not Hostile.] (Aftonbladet 16/1 1946.)

Interview by Carl Olof Bernhardsson with the new Minister of Commerce.

187 Zurück zum Welthandel. Auch kleine Länder können die internationale Handelsfreiheit fördern. (Schweizer Illustrierte Zeitung 1946: 19, p. 2.)
Interview.

1947

188 Det går framåt. [We Go Forward.] (Vi 34 (1947): 51/52, p. 6.)
The article deals with European problems.

189 Prospects of the Economic Commission for Europe. (United Nations Bulletin 3 (1947): July 29, pp. 147—149.)

190 [Foreword to:] The Economic Commission for Europe. Published by the Department of Public Information, United Nations, Lake Success, N. Y., 1947, pp. 2—3. (What the United Nations Is Doing.) [Cf. 213, 237, 270.]

191 The Role of the U. N. Economic Commission. (Export-Import Journal, August 1947.)

1948

192 The American Paradox. (The Crisis, September 1948, pp. 267—269, 285.)
Excerpts of 195.

193 * Contact met Amerika. [Orig. titles:] Kontakt med Amerika & Amerika mitt i världen. [With] Alva Myrdal. Vertaald door [Transl. by] D. Epinardus. Den Haag, De Kern, 1948, 203 pp. (Continenten—Landen—Volkeren 1.) [Cf. 98b, 104.]

194 Los efectos económicos de la política fiscal. [Orig. title:] Finanspolitikens ekonomiska verkningar. Trad. directa del sueco por Bengt Becker. Revisión y nota preliminar por Manuel de Torres. Prólogo por Manuel Orbea. Madrid, M. Aguilar, 1948, 408 pp. (Biblioteca de ciencias económicas, políticas y sociales.) [Cf. 44, 241, 360.]

195 Of American Democracy. [An Unedited Speech . . . June 2, 1948.] (Art and Action. 10th anniversary issue [of] Twice a Year . . . New York 1948, pp. 567—575.) [Cf. 192.]

Address at a dinner given in the author's honor by the Committee of 100 at the Waldorf Astoria Hotel in New York City, June 2, 1948.

196+ Social Trends in America and Strategic Approaches to the Negro problem. (Phylon 9 (1948), pp. 196—214.)

Paper read in honor of the Julius Rosenwald Fund in Chicago, May 28, 1948.

197 Vad gör Europakommissionen? [What Does the Economic Commission for Europe Do?] (Industria 44 (1948): 3, pp. 36—38, 66—67.)

198 [Foreword to:] Europas ekonomi efter kriget. En sammanfattning av FN:s ekonomiska Europakommissions rapport 1948. [The Economy of Europe after the War. A summary of the Report of the United Nations Economic Commission for Europe, 1948.] Stockholm 1948, pp. 7—10. [Cf. 200.]

199 [Foreword to:] Rose, Arnold: The Negro in America. A Condensation of An American Dilemma by Gunnar Myrdal. With the assistance of Richard Sterner and Arnold Rose. New York, Harper, [etc.] 1948, pp. XIII—XVII. [Cf. 127a.]

Other editions: London, Secker & Warburg, 1948; Boston, Beacon Press, 1956; New York, Harper & Row, 1964.

200 [Foreword to:] A Survey of the Economic Situation and Prospects of Europe. United Nations. Department of Economic Affairs. [Prepared by the] Research and Planning Division. Economic Commission for Europe. Geneva 1948, p. III. [Cf. 198.]

Also published in German [with the title: Lage und Aussichten der europäischen Wirtschaft. Ein Überblick . . . Köln 1949], French and Russian.

201 Forsiktig Optimisme for det europæiske økonomiske Samarbejde. [Cautious Optimism as to the Economic Collaboration in Europe.] (Randers Amtsavis 31/12 1948.)

27

1949

202 American Dilemma Still Remains in Our Intentions of Democracy and What We Do about Our Serious Race Problems. (Motive, January 1949, pp. 15—16, 44.) [Cf. 127a.]

203 L'E.C.E. e la cooperazione economica europea. Roma 1949. (La Comunità internazionale 4 (1949): 1, pp. 1—12.)

---

204 [Foreword to:] Economic Survey of Europe in 1948. United Nations. Department of Economic Affairs. Prepared by the Research and Planning Division. Economic Commission for Europe. Geneva 1949, p. III.

205 ECE — Europas økonomiraad. [ECE — The Economic Council of Europe.] (Information 24/6 1949.)

206 Progress Report on Europe. (United Nations World 3 (1949): June, pp. 54—55.)
Interview.

1950

207 Economic Commission for Europe. Proposals for Future Work Program. (United Nations Bulletin 8 (1950): May 15, pp. 422—427.) [Cf. 253.]

208 L'équilibre monétaire. [Orig. title:] Monetary Equilibrium. Avant-propos par André Marchal. Trad. de l'anglais par Béatrix Marchal. Paris, Librairie de Médicis, Génin, 1950, 211 pp. [Cf. 91c.]

209 Opening Speech by the Executive Secretary [Gunnar Myrdal], Economic Commission for Europe. Session 5. United Nations, Economic and Social Council. [Lake Success] 1950, 10 pp. (E/ECE/118. 31/5 1950.)

210 Report to the 5th Session of the E. C. E. by the Executive Secretary [Gunnar Myrdal] on the Future Work of the Commission. United Nations Economic Commission for Europe. Geneva, April 1950, 70 pp., 4 Appendices. (General E/ECE/114. Rev. 1.)

211 RX for Europe's Sick Economy. (United Nations World 4 (1950): June, pp. 28—30.)

212+ The Trend towards Economic Planning. (Festskrift tillägnad ... Gösta Eberstein sjuttioårsdagen den 4 december 1950. Stockholm 1950, pp. 175—211.) [Cf. 218—219.]
The Ludwig Mond Lecture, Manchester University, 13 March, 1950.

———

213 [Foreword to:] The Economic Commission for Europe. Published by the Department of Public Information, United Nations. New York . . . 1950, p. 1. (What the United Nations Is Doing.) [Cf. 190, 237.]

214 [Foreword to:] Economic Survey of Europe in 1949. United Nations. Department of Economic Affairs. Prepared by the Research and Planning Division. Economic Commission for Europe. Geneva 1950, pp. III—VII.

1951

215 Developments in All-European Economic Co-operation during 1950. (Uphill. Nine Leading Figures on the United Nations' Progress and Difficulties in 1950. Ed. by Stephen W. Pollak. London [1951?], pp. 35—42.)

216 Issues before the Economic Commission for Europe. (United Nations Bulletin 10 (1951): May 15, pp. 476—477.)

217 The Recognition of Man's Economic Rights. (Unesco Courier, Dec. 1951.)

218+ The Trend towards Economic Planning. [Ur: Festskrift tilläg-nad. . . Gösta Eberstein sjuttioårsdagen den 4 december 1950.] (The Manchester School of Economic and Social Studies 19 (1951), pp. 1—42.) [Cf. 212, 219.]

219 Utvecklingen mot planhushållning. [Orig. title: The Trend towards Economic Planning.] (Tiden 43 (1951), pp. 71—84, 134—150.) [Cf. 212, 218.]

1952

220 Les aspects économiques de la santé. [Orig. title: Economic Aspects of Health.] (Chronique de l'Organisation mondiale de santé 6 (1952): 7/8, pp. 224—242. [Off-print, pp. 14—32.] — Revue économique 6 (1952), pp. 785—804.) [Cf. 221.]

221 Economic Aspects of Health. (Chronicle of the World Health Organization 6 (1952). 7/0, pp. 203—218. [Off-print, pp. 13—28.]) [Cf. 220.]
Lecture at the Fifth World Health Assembly, Geneva, 1952.

222 Proved Instrument of European Economic Cooperation. (United Nations Bulletin 12 (1952): March 15, pp. 262—264.)

223⁺ Psychological Impediments to Effective International Cooperation. (The Journal of Social Issues. Suppl. ser. No. 6. 1952, pp. 5—31.) [Cf. 229, 234, 520.]
Kurt Lewin Memorial Award Issue. — Kurt Lewin Memorial Lecture in the American Psychological Association and the Society for the Psychological Study of Social Issues.

1953

224 Achievements at ECE Session. (United Nations Bulletin 14 (1953): April 15, pp. 279—280.)

225 Das gestörte Gleichgewicht der Weltwirtschaft. Zur Problematik der „unterentwickelten Gebiete". (Aussenpolitik 4 (1953): H. 1, pp. 19—26.)

226 Gustav Cassel 1866—1944 [!]. (Stora nationalekonomer. [Av] Joseph Schumpeter ... Stockholm 1953, pp. 341—353.) [Cf. 155, 394, 464.]

227 Hur ECE bidrar till Europas ekonomiska hälsa. [How ECE Contributes to the Economical Health of Europe.] (Världshorisont 1953: 10, pp. 17—19, 32.)

228a⁺The Political Element in the Development of Economic Theory. [Orig. title: Vetenskap och politik i nationalekonomien.] Transl. from the German [Das politische Element in der nationalökonomischen Doktrinbildung] by Paul Streeten.

[With author's new Preface and] Appendix: Recent Controversies. By Paul Streeten. London, Routledge & Kegan Paul, 1953, XVIII, 248 pp. (International Library of Sociology and Social Reconstruction.) [Cf. 11c, 26, 233.]
Apart from a few cuts and minor editorial rearrangements, the English edition is an unrevised translation of the original Swedish version. — Several later repr.

228b — Cambridge, Mass., 1954. (233)

228c — New York 1969. (715)

229 Psykologiska hinder för effektiv internationell samverkan. [Orig. title: Psychological Impediments to Effective International Cooperation.] 1—2. (Tiden 45 (1953), pp. 132—145; 197—209.) [Cf. 223.]

230+ The Relation between Social Theory and Social Policy. (The British Journal of Sociology 4 (1953), pp. 210—242.) [Cf. 235—236, 264, 292, 299, 590.]
Opening Address at the Conference of the British Sociological Association, March 27, 1953.

————————

231 Människans ekonomiska rättigheter. [The Human Rights in the Economical Field.] (Arbetet 7/7 1953.)
Also published in other newspapers.

1954

232 Advancing Economic Cooperation on an All-European Scale. An Appraisal of the Positive Results of ECE's 9th Session. (United Nations Bulletin 16 (1954), pp. 346—347.)

233 The Political Element in the Development of Economic Theory. [Orig. title: Vetenskap och politik i nationalekonomien.] Transl. from the German by Paul Streeten ... Cambridge, Mass., Harvard University Press, 1954, XVIII, 248 pp. [Cf. 11c, 26, 228b.]
Repr. 1961, 1965, 1971.

234 Psychological Impediments to Effective International Cooperation. (American Journal of International Law 48 (1954), pp. 304—307.) [Cf. 223.]

235 La relazione tra la teoria sociale et la politica sociale. [Orig. title: The Relation Between Social Theory and Social Policy.] [Transl. by Anna Bagiotti Craveri.](La rivista internazionale di scienze economiche e commerciali 1 (1954), pp. 46—80. [Off-print Padova 1954, 35 pp.]) [Cf. 230.]

236 Social teori och socialpolitik. [Social Theory and Social Policy.] 1—3. (Sociala meddelanden 1954: 2—4, pp. 63—75, 131—140, 211—223.) [Cf. 230.]
Introductory lecture at the Conference of the British Sociological Association in London, 1953. Transl. by Olle Moberg and rev. by Leif Björk.

---

237 [Foreword to:] The Economic Commission for Europe. Published by the United Nations Department of Public Information. New York ... 1954, pp. 1—2. (What the United Nations Is Doing . . .) [Cf. 190, 213.]

1955

238+ Realities and Illusions in Regard to Inter-Governmental Organizations. London 1955, Geoffrey Cumberlege, Oxford University Press, 1955, 28 pp. (L. T. Hobhouse Memorial Trust Lecture 24.)
Lecture, 25 February, 1954, at Bedford College, London.

239+ Toward a More Closely Integrated Free-World Economy. (National Policy for Economic Welfare at Home and Abroad. Ed. by Robert Lekachman. Garden City, N. Y., 1955, pp. 235—292 = Columbia University. Bicentennial Conference Series . . .)

1956

240+ Development and Under-Development. A Note on the Mechanism of National and International Economic Inequality. Cairo, N. B. E. Printing Press, 1956, 88 pp. [Cf. 255a, 647.]
National Bank of Egypt. Fiftieth Anniversary Commemoration Lectures. — 1st Lecture: The Quest for a Theory of Economic Development and Under-Development. — 2nd Lecture: The Cumulative Process of Economic Development within a National State. — 3rd Lecture: The

241 Los efectos económicos de la política fiscal. [Orig. title:] Finanspolitikens ekonomiska verkningar. Trad. directa del sueco por Bengt Becker. Rev. y nota preliminar por Manuel de Torres. Prólogo por Manuel Orbea. 2ª ed. Madrid, M. Aguilar, 1956, 360 pp. [Cf. 194.]

242 Den europeiska öst-väst-handeln inom världsekonomiens ram. [The European East-West Trade in World Economy.] (Nationalekonomiska Föreningens Förhandlingar 3 okt. 1956, pp. 85—114 [incl. discussion].)
Lecture at the meeting of the Society of Political Economy (Stockholm), 3 Oct., 1956.

243⁺ An International Economy. Problems and Prospects. [With] Appendix: Methodological Note on the Concepts and the Value Premises. New York, Harper & Brothers, 1956, XIV, 381 pp. [Cf. 244a—c.]

244a — London, Routledge & Kegan Paul, 1956, XIV, 381 pp. [Cf. 243.]

244b — New York/London & Tokyo 1964. (416)

244c — New York 1969. (706)

244d Translations.
[French:] Une économie internationale. Paris 1958. (278)
[German:] Internationale Wirtschaft. Berlin 1958. (284)
[Russian:] Mirovaja ėkonomika. Moskva 1958. (287)
[Spanish:] Solidaridad o desintegración. México & Buenos Aires 1956 . . . (246a—c)
[Swedish:] Världsekonomin. Stockholm 1956. (247)
[—] —Stockholm 1969. (728)
[Tamil:] Pannattu Poruladharam. New Delhi 1973. (946)

245⁺ The Research Work of the Secretariat of the Economic Commission for Europe. (25 Economic Essays . . . in honour of Erik Lindahl, 21 November, 1956. Stockholm 1956, pp. 267—293. [Off-print 1956, 27 pp.])

246a Solidaridad o desintegración. Tendencias actuales de las relaciones económicas internacionales en el mundo no soviético. [Orig. title:] An International Economy. Problems and Prospects. Trad. de Salvador Echavarría y Enrique González Pedrero. México & Buenos Aires, Fondo de cultura económica, 1956, 455 pp. [Cf. 244d.]

246b — 2ª ed. México & Buenos Aires 1962. (370)

246c — 3ª ed. México & Buenos Aires 1966. (522)

247 Världsekonomin. Övers. från förf:s engelska manuskript av Leif Björk. [An International Economy. Transl. from the author's English manuscript by . . .] Stockholm, Tiden, 1956, 487 pp. [Cf. 244d, 728.]

---

248 [Foreword to:] Wright, Richard: The Color Curtain. A Report on the Bandung Conference. Cleveland & New York 1956, pp. 7—8. [Cf. 271.]

1957

249 A Challenge. (255a: Economic Theory and Under-Developed Regions, pp. 98—104. — 265: Rich Lands and Poor . . ., pp. 100—106.)

250 Comercio internacional y ayuda a paises subdesarrollados. [Orig. title: Trade and Aid.] (Economía internacional 2 (1957): sept./oct., pp. 8—24.) [Cf. 268.]

251 The Conservative Predilections of Economic Theory and Their Foundation in the Basic Philosophies. (255a: Economic Theory and Under-Developed Regions, pp. 135—146. — 265: Rich Lands and Poor . . ., pp. 137—149.)

252 The Drift toward Regional Economic Inequalities in a Country. (255a: Economic Theory and Under-Developed Regions, pp. 23—38. — 265: Rich Lands and Poor . . ., pp. 23—38.) [Identical with 816.]

253 The Economic Commission for Europe. (United Nations Review 4 (1957): July, pp. 24—25, 56—61.) [Cf. 207.]

254 Economic Nationalism and Internationalism. (The Australian Outlook 11 (1957): 4, pp. 3—50. [Off-print. Melbourne 1957, 50 pp.])
The Dyason Lectures, 1957.

255a⁺ Economic Theory and Under-Developed Regions. London, Duckworth, 1957, XII, 167 pp.
Contents: 1. An Unexplained General Trait of Social Reality. (269) — 2. The Principle of Circular and Cumulative Causation. (263) — 3. The Drift towards Regional Economic Inequalities in a Country. (252) — 4. The Role of the State. (267) — 5. International Inequalities. (257) — 6. National State Policies in Under-Developed Countries. (260) — 7. National Economic Planning in Under-Developed Countries. (259) — 8. A Challenge. (249) — 9. The Equality Doctrine and the Escape from It. (256) — 10. The Conservative Predilections of Economic Theory and Their Foundation in the Basic Philosophies. (251) — 11. A Note on the Theory of International Trade and the Inequality Problem. (261) — 12. The Logical Crux of All Science. (258)

A revision of Development and Underdevelopment. (240) — American ed. with the title: Rich Lands and Poor. (265) — Several repr.

255b — Bombay 1958. (277)

255c — London 1963. (390)

255d — New York . . . 1971. (794)

255e Translations.
[Arabian:] al-Bilād al-ghanīyah wal-faqīrah. al-Qāhirah 1962. (357)
[—] al-Naẓarīyah al-iqtiṣādīyah wa-al-duwal al-nāmīyah. al-Qāhirah 1964. (421)
[Danish:] Verdens økonomiske ulighed. København 1958. (301)
[French:] Théorie économique et pays sousdéveloppés. Paris 1959. (321)
[German:] Ökonomische Theorie und unterentwickelte Regionen. Stuttgart 1959. (310)
[—] — Weltproblem Armut. Frankfurt am Main 1974. (996)
[Italian:] Teoria economica e paesi sottosviluppati. Milano 1959. (318)
[—] — Milano 1966. (524)

[Japanese:] Keizai-riron to teikaihatsu chi-iki. Tōkyō 1959. (307)
[Korean:] Chŏgae-palguk-ŭi kyŏngje iron. Sŏul [1960]. (324)
[—] Kyŏngje iron-gwa chŏgaebal chiyŏk. Seoul 1972. (A34)
[Persian:] Ti'ūrī-ji iqtiṣādī va kišvarhā-ji kam-rušd. Tihrān 1966, 1971. (525, 822)
[Polish:] Teoria ekonomii a kraje gospodarczo nierozwinięte. Warszawa 1958. (295)
[Portuguese:] Teoria econômica e regiões subdesenvolvidas. Rio de Janeiro 1960. (327)
[—] — Rio de Janeiro 1965. (478)
[Spanish:] Teoría económica y regiones subdesarrolladas. México & Buenos Aires 1959. (319)
[—] — 2ª ed. México & Buenos Aires 1964. (435)
[Swedish:] Ekonomisk teori och underutvecklade regioner. Stockholm 1969. (702)
[—] Rika och fattiga länder. Stockholm 1957. (266)

256 The Equality Doctrine and the Escape from It. (255a: Economic Theory and Under-Developed Regions, pp. 107—134. — 265: Rich Lands and Poor . . ., pp. 109—136.)

257 International Inequalities. (255a: Economic Theory and Under-Developed Regions, pp. 50—65. — 265: Rich Lands and Poor . . ., pp. 50—66.) [Cf. 417, 654.]

258 The Logical Crux of All Science. (255a: Economic Theory and Under-Developed Regions, pp. 159—164. — 265: Rich Lands and Poor . . ., pp. 163—168.) [Cf. 286, 299, 308, 994.]

259 National Economic Planning in Underdeveloped Countries. (255a: Economic Theory and Under-Developed Regions, pp. 79—97. — 265: Rich Lands and Poor . . ., pp. 81—99.)

260 National State Policies in Underdeveloped Countries. (255a: Economic Theory and Under-Developed Regions, pp. 66—78. — 265: Rich Lands and Poor . . ., pp. 67—80.) [Cf. 420.]

261 A Note on the Theory of International Trade and the Inequality Problem. (255a: Economic Theory and Under-Developed Regions, pp. 147—158. — 265: Rich Lands and Poor . . ., pp. 150—162.)

262 Opening Statement by the Executive Secretary, Gunnar Myrdal, to the 12th session of the Economic Commission for Europe, 29/4, 1957. United Nations, Economic and Social Council. [Geneva] 1957, 18 pp. (E/ECE/287.)

263 The Principle of Circular and Cumulative Causation. (255a: Economic Theory and Under-Developed Regions, pp. 11—22. — 265: Rich Lands and Poor . . ., pp. 11—22.) [Cf. 815.]

264 Il rapporto tra la teoria e la politica sociale. [Orig. title:] The Relation Between Social Theory and Social Policy.] [Trad. by Giulia Sanvisenti.] (Repr. from L'Industria 1957: 1, 43 pp.) [Cf. 230.]

265 Rich Lands and Poor. The Road to World Prosperity. New York, Harper & Brothers, [1957], XX, 168 pp. (World Perspectives. Planned and ed. by Ruth Nanda Anshen. 16.) [Cf. 389, 917.]
Original English ed. with the title: Economic Theory and Under-Developed Regions. (255a)

266 Rika och fattiga länder. [Orig. title: Economic Theory and Underdeveloped Regions.] Övers. [Transl.]: James Rössel. Stockholm, Tiden, 1957, 218 pp. [Cf. 255e, 702.]

267 The Role of the State. (255a: Economic Theory and Under-Developed Regions, pp. 39—49. — 265: Rich Lands and Poor . . ., pp. 39—49.)

268+ Trade and Aid. (The American Scholar 26 (1957), pp. 137—154.) [Cf. 250, 297, 328.]
Address at the New School for Social Research, New York, 8 December, 1956. Contribution to a Symposium on Welfare Democracy and its International Importance.

269 An Unexplained General Trait of Social Reality. (255a: Economic Theory and Under-Developed Regions, pp. 3—10. — 265: Rich Lands and Poor . . ., pp. 3—10.)

---

270 [Foreword to:] ECE. The First Ten Years. 1947—1957. United Nations Economic Commission for Europe. Geneva 1957, pp. 1—3. (E/ECE/291.) [Stencil.] [Cf. 190.]

271 [Foreword to:] Wright, Richard: De kleurbarrière. Een verslag van de Conferentie van Bandung. 's-Gravenhage 1957, pp. [Cf. 248.]

272 De internationella ekonomiska organisationerna. [International Organizations in the Economic Field.] (Svenska Dagbladet 15/10 1957.) [Cf. 273.]

273 Det internationella samarbetets brister. [Shortcomings of the International Cooperation.] (Svenska Dagbladet 22/10 1957.) [Cf. 272.]

274 Underutvecklade länder: hjälpverksamheten. [Underdeveloped Countries: the Aid Activity.] [1—2.] (Svenska Dagbladet 8/2, 14/2 1957.)

275 Private Lives: No. 3. In Which a Celebrity Speaks his Mind on a Topic of his Own Choice. By Gunnar Myrdal. (Sydney Morning Herald, Sept. 7, 1957.)
Interview

1958

276 American Ideals and the American Conscience. (299: Value in Social Theory, pp. 65—70.) [Cf. 846.]
A brief summary of Chapter 1 of An American Dilemma. (127a)

277 Economic Theory and Under-Developed Regions. Authorised Indian ed. Bombay, Vora & Co., 1958, 183 pp. [Cf. 255b.]

278 Une économie internationale. Trad. française de: An International Economy. Paris, Presses universitaires de France, 1958, VIII, 506 pp. (Théoria 10.) [Cf. 244d.]

279[1] Encountering the Negro Problem. (299: Value in Social Theory, pp. 89—118.) [Cf. 361.]
An American Dilemma. Chapter 2, pp. 26—49. (127a)

279[2] Ends and Means in Political Economy. Transl. from the German [Das Zweck-Mittel-Denken in der Nationalökonomie] by the Editor [Paul Streeten]. (299: Value in Social Theory, pp. 206—230.) [Cf. 42.]

280 Facets of the Negro Problem. (299: Value in Social Theory,. pp. 165—197.) [Cf. 797.]
Summaries of sections of Chapter 3 of An American Dilemma, pp. 50—80. (127a)

281 Facts and Valuations [in Social Science]. (299: Value in Social Theory, pp. 119—164.)
An American Dilemma. Appendix 2: A Methodological Note on Facts and Valuations in Social Science, pp. 1035—1064. (127a)

282 Indian Economic Planning. (United Asia 10 (1958): 4 [= special number entitled An Evaluation Report on the 2nd Five Year Plan], pp. 272—281.)
Address to Members of Parliament [New Delhi], April 22, 1958. — The article differs very little from Indian Economic Planning in Its Broader Setting. [Cf. 306.]

283 International Integration. 1: The Place of Value Premises in Scientific Analysis. — 2: The Classical Theory of the Perfect Market. — 3: The Classical Theory of International Trade. (299: Value in Social Theory, pp. 1—8.)
An International Economy ... Appendix. Methodological Note on the Concepts and the Value Premises. The Place of Value Premises in Scientific Analysis ..., pp. 336—340. (243)

284 Internationale Wirtschaft. Probleme und Aussichten. [Orig. title:] An International Economy. Problems and Prospects. Aus dem Englischen übertr. von Ben Lehbert und D. Anderson. Berlin, Duncker & Humblot, 1958, 436 pp. [Cf. 244d.]

285 Introduction to the Study of the Negro Problem. (299: Value in Social Theory, pp. 55—64.)
An American Dilemma. Introduction. 1. The Negro Problem as a Moral Issue. — 2. Valuations and Beliefs, pp. XLI—XLVII. (127a)

286 The Logical Crux of All Science. (299: Value in Social Theory, pp. 231—236.) [Cf. 258.]

287 Mirovaja ėkonomika. Problemy i perspektivy. [Orig. title: An International Economy. Problems and Prospects.] Perev. s anglijskogo A. V. Evrejskova i O. G. Klesmet. Vstup. stat'ja A. I. Bečina. Red. Ju. Ja. Ol'sevič. Moskva, Izd. Inostrannoj literatury, 1958, 556 pp. [Cf. 244d.]

288 Need for Population Control in India. (Swasth Hind 2 (1958), pp. 245—246.)

Extract from the author's address to the Indian Parliament [New Delhi], in April, 1958.

289 The Principle of Cumulation. (299: Value in Social Theory, pp. 198—205.) [Cf. 426, 473.]

An American Dilemma. Appendix 3. A Methodological Note on the Principle of Cumulation, pp. 1065—1070. (127a)

290 El problema de la eficiencia de la mano de obra en los paises subdesarrollados. [Versión de Óscar Soberón.] (El trimestre económico 25 (1958), pp. 749—769.) [Cf. 312.]

291 Rational Approach to Social Reality. (Bulletin of the Ramakrishna Mission Institute of Culture 9 (1958): July, pp. 159—164.)

292 The Relation Between Social Theory and Social Policy. (299: Value in Social Theory, pp. 9—54.) [Cf. 230.]

293+ The Role of the Price Mechanism in Planning for Economic Development of Underdeveloped Countries. ([Festskrift] Til Frederik Zeuthen 9 sept. 1958. København 1958, pp. 257—273 = Nationaløkonomisk Tidsskrift. 96. Tillægshefte.) [Not identical with 314.]

294 Social Needs in Underdeveloped Countries and their Resources to Meet Them. 22 pp. [Cf. 305, 313—314, 317.]

Opening Address to the Ninth International Conference of Social Work in Tokyo, December 1, 1958.

295 Teoria ekonomii a kraje gospodarczo nierozwinięte. [Orig. title:] Economic Theory and Under-Developed Regions. Tłumaczył z angielskiego Stanisław Ficowski. Warszawa, Polskie Wydawnictwa Gospodarcze, 1958, 216 pp. [Cf. 255e.]

296 Tiden och partiet. [Tiden and the Party.] (Tiden. Tidskrift för socialistisk kritik och politik. En minnesskrift . . . Stockholm 1958, pp. 129—138.) [Cf. 162.]

297 Trade and Aid. (Readings in International Politics: Concepts and Issues. Ed. by Charles O. Lerche, Jr., and Margaret E. Lerche. New York 1958, pp. 305—313.) [Cf. 268.]

298 Valuations and Beliefs. (299: Value in Social Theory, pp. 71—88.)
An American Dilemma. Appendix 1. A Methodological Note on Valuations and Beliefs, pp. 1027—1034. (127a)

299+ Value in Social Theory. A Selection of Essays on Methodology. Ed. by Paul Streeten. London, Routledge & Kegan Paul, 1958, XLVI, 269 pp. [Cf. 300a.]
Contents: Introduction by Paul Streeten. — International Integration. (283) — The Relation between Social Theory and Social Policy. (292) — Introduction to the Study of the Negro Problem. (285) — American Ideals and the American Conscience. (276) — Valuations and Beliefs. (298) — Encountering the Negro Problem. (279¹) — Facts and Valuations. (281) — Facets of the Negro Problem. (280) — The Principle of Cumulation. (289) — Ends and Means in Political Economy. (279²) — The Logical Crux of All Science. (258) — Postscript.

Repr. 1962 and 1968.

300a — New York, Harper & Brothers, 1958, XLVI, 269 pp. [Appendix. See 826: Vetenskap och politik i nationalekonomin, pp. 265—289.] [Cf. 299.]

300b Translations.
[German:] Das Wertproblem in der Sozialwissenschaft. Hannover 1965. (491)
[Italian:] Il valore nella teoria sociale. Torino 1966. (530)
[Portuguese:] O valor em teoria social. São Paulo 1965. (485)

301 Verdens økonomiske ulighed. Overs. af [Transl. by] Lars Andersen efter "Economic Theory and Underdeveloped Regions". København, Det Danske Forlag, 1958, 191 pp. [Cf. 255e.]

_____

302 India's Economy: Need for Rapid Progress. (The Hindu 17/7 1958.) [Continuation of 303.]

303 Need for Flexibility in Planning. (The Hindu 15/7 1958.) [Continued by 302.]

1959

304 Gli assunti teorici della pianificazione sociale. (Sociologia: applicazioni e richerche. Bari 1959, pp. 243—264. (Biblioteca di cultura moderna 541.))

305 Les besoins sociaux dans les pays sous-développés et les ressources dont ils disposent pour y faire face. (Informations sociales 13 (1959): Août/sept., pp. 24—37.) [Cf. 294.]

306+ Indian Economic Planning in Its Broader Setting. (Population Review. Journal of Asian Democracy 3 (1959), pp. 17—32. [Off-print published by The Secretary, Congress Party in Parliament, New Delhi. [1958], 30 pp.]) [Cf. 282.]
Address to Members of Parliament [New Delhi], April 22, 1958.

307 Keizai-riron to teikaihatsu chi-iki. [Japanese transl. of: Economic Theory and Under-Developed Regions.] [Transl. by:] Keiji Ohara. Tōkyō, Toyo Keizi Shimpo Sha, 1959, X, 208, 6 pp. [Cf. 255e.]

308 Das logische Kreuz aller Wissenschaft. [Orig. title: The Logical Crux of All Science.] (310: Ökonomische Theorie und unterentwickelte Regionen, pp. 157—162.) [Cf. 258.]

309 Note on Comments to the National Planning Council at its meeting of 11 March 1958 on Planning and Related Matters. (Papers by Visiting Economists. National Planning Council Secretariat. Colombo, Ceylon, 1959, pp. 119—123.)

310 Ökonomische Theorie und unterentwickelte Regionen. Übers. nach der englischen Originalausg. "Economic Theory and Under-Developed Regions" von Ben Lehbert. Stuttgart, Gustav Fischer, 1959, XII, 162 pp. [Cf. 255e.]

311 Il problema del valore. (Pagani, A.: Scienza sociale e politica sociale. Bologna 1959, pp. 29—35.)
Italian transl. of the Value Problem = Value in Social Theory. 1958, pp. 48—54. [Cf. 299.]

312 Il problema dell'efficienza della mano d'opera nei paesi sottosviluppati. (Informazioni Svimez 8 (1959), pp. 2330—2342.) [Cf. 290.]

313 Resources to Meet Social Needs in Underdeveloped countries. (United Asia 11 (1959), pp. 16—22.) [Cf. 294.]
Adaptation of Opening Address to the Ninth International Conference of Social Work in Tokyo, December 1, 1958.

314 The Role of the Price Mechanism in Economic Planning in the Underdeveloped Countries. (The Bulletin of the International House of Japan, Inc. Winter, 1959: 3, pp. 16—22.) [Not identical with 293.] [Cf. 294.]
Adaptation of Opening Address to the Ninth International Conference of Social Work in Tokyo, December 1, 1958.

315 Saúde pública e desenvolvimento econômico. Conferência. (Econômica brasileira 5 (1959): 3/4, pp. 69—81.)

316 La selezione delle premesse di valore. (Pagani, A.: Scienza sociale e politica sociale. Bologna 1959, pp. 36—44.)
Italian transl. from Value in Social Theory. 1958, pp. 157—162. [Cf. 299.]

317 Soziale Bedürfnisse in unterentwickelten Ländern und ihre Hilfsmöglichkeiten, sie zu befriedigen. (Nachrichtendienst des Deutschen Vereins für öffentliche und private Fürsorge, Frankfurt am Main. 1959: 7, pp. 220—224.) [Cf. 294.]

318 Teoria economica e paesi sottosviluppati. [Orig. title:] Economic Theory and Under-Developed Regions. Trad. di Elisa Marengo e Vincenzo Vitello. Milano 1959, Feltrinelli, 212 pp. [Cf. 255e, 524.]

319 Teoría económica y regiones subdesarrolladas. [Orig. title:] Economic Theory and Under-Developed Regions. Trad. de Ernesto Cuesta y Óscar Soberón. México & Buenos Aires, Fondo de cultura económica, 1959, 189 pp. [Cf. 255e, 435.]

320 Theoretical Assumptions of Social Planning. (World Congress of Sociology [Milan and Stresa, 8—15 September, 1959]. Transactions 1959: 2, pp. 155—167.)

321 Théorie économique et pays sous-développés. [Orig. title: Economic Theory and Under-Developed Regions.] Trad. de l'anglais par J. Chazelle. Paris, Présence africaine, 1959, 192 pp. (Enquêtes et études.)[Cf. 255e.]

1960

322+ Beyond the Welfare State. Economic Planning and Its International Implications. New Haven & London, Yale University Press, 1960, 287 pp. [Cf. 323a—d, 385, 425, 527.]
The Storrs Lectures in Jurisprudence, 1958. — Several repr.

323a — Economic Planning in the Welfare States and Its International Implications. London, Duckworth, 1960, XIV, 214 pp. [Cf. 322.]

323b — Economic Planning and Its International Implications. New Haven & London 1965. (453)

323c — Economic Planning in the Welfare States and Its International Implications. London 1965. (454)

323d — Economic Planning and Its International Implications. New York, Toronto & London 1967. (559)

323e Translations.
[Catalan:] Perspectives de la planificació. Barcelona 1965. (472)
[Dutch:] De toekomst van de welvaartsstaat. Amsterdam 1963. (402)
[French:] Planifier pour développer. Paris 1963. (398)
[German:] Jenseits des Wohlfahrtstaates. Stuttgart 1961. (335)
[Italian:] I paesi del benessere e gli altri. Milano 1962. (368)
[Japanese:] Fukushi kokka wo koete. Tōkyō 1963. (392)
[—] — Tōkyō 1970. (748)
[Korean:] Hyŏndae pokchi kukkaron. Seoul 1972. (A34)
[Portuguese:] O estado do futuro. Rio de Janeiro 1962. (362)
[Spanish:] El estado del futuro. México & Buenos Aires 1961. (331a—b)
[—] — México & Buenos Aires 1963. (391[1])
[Swedish:] Planhushållning i välfärdsstaten. Stockholm 1961. (340)

324 Chŏgae-palguk-ŭi kyŏngje iron. [Korean transl. of: Economic Theory and Under-Developed Regions.] Sŏul 4293 [= 1960], 195 pp. [Cf. 255e.]

325 National versus International Integration. (America's Foreign Policy. Ed. . . . by Harold Karan Jacobson. New York 1960, pp. 188—212.)

326 La scienza delle finanze. [Orig. title: The Theory of Public Finance.] (Storia e storiografia del pensiero finanziario. Scritti . . . Ristampa a cura del dott. Antonio Li Calzi. Padova 1960, pp. 217—266.)
Italian transl. of Chapter 7 of The Political Element in the Development of Economic Theory. [Cf. 233.]

327 Teoria econômica e regiões subdesenvolvidas. [Orig. title:] Economic Theory and Under-Developed Regions. [Trad. de Ewaldo Corrêa Lima; revista por Neusa Feital Wöhrle e Célio Lyra.] Rio de Janeiro 1960, 210 pp. (Textos de economia contemporânea 1.) [Cf. 255e, 478.]

328 Trade and Aid. (The Underdeveloped Lands. A Dilemma of the International Economy. Comp. and ed. by DeVere E. Pentony. San Francisco 1960, pp. 69—84.) [Cf. 268.]

1961

329 Bjælken i vort eget øje. [The Beam in Our Eyes.][Velfærdsstat — velfærdsverden 3.] (Andelsbladet 62 (1961), pp. 217—220.) [1—2 see 346, 338. Cf. 330.]

330 Bjälken i vårt öga. [The Beam in Our Eyes.] [Välfärdsstat — välfärdsvärld 3.] (Vi 48 (1961): 8, pp. 18, 36—37.) [1—2 see 343, 337. Cf. 329.]

331a El estado del futuro. [Orig. title:] Beyond the Welfare State. Trad. de Florentino M. Torner. México & Buenos Aires, Fondo de cultura económica, 1961, 295 pp. (Tiempo presente 25.) [Cf. 323e, 359.]

331b — 2ª ed. México & Buenos Aires 1963. (391¹)

332 FN bättre än rikemansklubb. [UN Better than a Rich Men's Club.] (Vi 48 (1961): 18, pp. 14—15, 62.)
Inför världsrevolutionen [2]. [1, 3—4 see 334, 344, 339.]

333 Hur har det lyckats? [How Did It Turn Out?] (Femton år med Tage Erlander. En skrift till 60-årsdagen 13 juni 1961. Red. av Olle Svensson. Stockholm 1961, pp. 7—18.) [Cf. 351.]

334 Inför världsrevolutionen. [On the Eve of the World Revolution.] [1.] (Vi 48 (1961): 17, pp. 20—21, 33—34.) [2—4 see 332, 344, 339.]
Address to a Swedish governmental commission for aid to underdeveloped countries.

335 Jenseits des Wohlfahrtsstaates. Wirtschaftsplanung in den Wohlfahrtsstaaten und ihre internationalen Folgen. [Orig. title:] Beyond the Welfare State. Übers. . . . von Ben Lehbert. Stuttgart, Gustav Fischer, 1961, XV, 227 pp. [Cf. 323e.]

336 Lever vi i ständigt uppror mot våra innersta ideal? [Do We Live in Permanent Revolt against Our Innermost Ideals?] (Fönstret 38 (1961), pp. 88—89.)
Excerpt from Planhushållning i välfärdsstaten, pp. 168—172. (340)

337 Den nödvändiga nationalismen. [The Necessary Nationalism.] [Välfärdsstat — välfärdsvärld 2.] (Vi 48 (1961): 7, pp. 13, 26—27.) [1, 3 see 343, 330.] [Cf. 338.]

338 Den nødvendige nationalisme. [The Necessary Nationalism.] [Velfærdsstat — velfærdsverden 2.] (Andelsbladet 62 (1961), pp. 187—189.) [1, 3 see 346, 329.] [Cf. 337.]

339 På budgeten eller genom insamlingar. [On the Budget or through Subscription.] (Vi 48 (1961): 20, pp. 23—24, 37.)
Inför världsrevolutionen [4]. [1—3 see 334, 332, 344.]

340 Planhushållning i välfärdsstaten. [Orig. title: Beyond the Welfare State.] Övers. av [Transl. by] James Rössel. Stockholm, Tiden 1961, 259 pp. [Cf. 323e, 336.]

341+ Problemet Sverige hjälper. [The Problem of Swedish Assistance [to Underdeveloped Countries].] Stockholm, Utrikespolitiska Institutet, 1961, 63 pp. (Världspolitikens dagsfrågor 1961: 7—8.) [Identical with 430.]

342 Den stora världsrevolutionen. [The Great World Revolution.] (Frihet 1961: 4, pp. 20—21, 46.) [Cf. 353.]

343 Välfärdsstat — välfärdsvärld. [Welfare State — Welfare World.] [1.] (Vi 48 (1961): 6, pp. 5—6.) [2—3 see 337, 330.] [Cf. 346.]

344 Välgörenhet är en ömtålig sak. [Charity Is a Delicate Matter.] (Vi 48 (1961): 19, pp. 17—18, 38—40.)
Inför världsrevolutionen [3]. [1—2, 4 see 334, 332, 339.]

345+ "Value-loaded" Concepts. (Money, Growth, and Methodology . . . In honor of Johan Åkerman, March 31, 1961 = Lund Social Science Studies 20. Lund 1961, pp. 273—288.)

346 Velfærdsstat — velfærdsverden. [Welfare State — Welfare World.] [1.] (Andelsbladet 62 (1961), pp. 159—161, 187—189.) [2—3 see 338, 329.] [Cf. 343.]

---

347 [Foreword to:] Nair, Kusum: Blossoms in the Dust. The Human Element in Indian Development. London 1961, pp. XIII—XVI. [Cf. 374¹.]

348 Axel Wenner-Gren. (Svenska Dagbladet 26/11 1961.)
Obituary.

349+ Dag Hammarskjöld myt för en ny tids människor. [D. H. a Myth for Modern Man.] (Aftonbladet 24/9 1961.)
Address to Students' Memorial Meeting.

350 Hälsohjälp — överbefolkning. [Health Assistance and Surplus Population.] (Länstidningen, Östersund, 21/10 1961.)

351 Hur har det lyckats? [How Did It Turn Out?] (Aftonbladet 10/6 1961.) [Cf. 333.]

352 Mat må komme først — industri sist. [Food First — Then Industry.] (Arbeiderbladet 13/6 1961 = Arbeiderbladets kronikk.)
The article is considered as Nr. 3 of a trilogy. 1—2 see 353.

353 Vi er inne i den store verdensrevolusjonen. [We Are in the Great World Revolution.] [1]—2. (Arbeiderbladet 10/6, 12/6 1961 = Arbeiderbladets kronikk.) [Cf. 342, 352.]

1962

354 An American Dilemma. (Race Vol. 4: 1. 1962, pp. 1—11.)
Address to Howard University, Washington, D.C., at the university's 94th Annual Commencement, June 8, 1962, with certain extracts from the preface to the Twentieth Anniversary Edition of An American Dilemma. [Cf. 355, 358, 378, 388.]

355 An American Dilemma. The Negro Problem and Modern Democracy. With the assistance of Richard Sterner and Arnold Rose. [With Author's Preface to the Twentieth Anniversary Edition and Postscript Twenty Years Later . . . by Arnold Rose.] New York & Evanston, Harper & Row, 1962, LXXXIII, 1483 pp. [Cf. 127b.]

356 Behovet av rebeller. [The Need of Rebels.] (Socialisten i tjugonde seklet 1962: 2—3, pp. 19—20.) [Not identical with 827.]

357 al-Bilād al-ghanīyah wal-faqīrah. [Arabian transl. of Economic Theory and Under-Developed Regions.] al-Qāhirah, Dār al-Qawmīyah, 1962, 146 pp. [Cf. 255e.]

358 The Commencement Address [on the Changing Status of the Negro]. (The Howard University Magazine 4 (1962): 4, pp. 4—9.) [Identical with 354, 388.] [Cf. 369, 378.]

359 Una controversia anticuada y confusa. (Balance 1/3 1962, pp. 16—18.)
The article corresponds to: El estado del futuro. Introducción, pp. 15—27. (331)

360 Los efectos económicos de la política fiscal. [Orig. title:] Finanspolitikens ekonomiska verkningar. Trad. del sueco por Bengt Becker. Revisión y nota preliminar por Manuel de Torres. Prólogo por Manuel Orbea ... 3ª ed. Madrid, Aguilar, 1962, XXVIII, 360 pp. (Biblioteca de ciencias sociales. Sección 1. Economía.) [Cf. 194.]

361 Encountering the Negro Problem. (The American Political Arena. Selected Readings. Ed. by Joseph R. Fiszman. Boston & Toronto 1962, pp. 534—540.) [Cf. 279.]
Abridged version from An American Dilemma, pp. 26—32. (127a)

362 O estado do futuro. [Orig. title: Beyond the Welfare State.] Trad. por Affonso Blacheyre. Rio de Janeiro, Zahar, 1962, 278 pp. [Cf. 323e.]

363 Folkets medlevande. [Popular Participation.] (Fönstret 39 (1962) [Jubileumsnummer], pp. 24—25.)

364 Internationella aspekter på de underutvecklade ländernas problem. Foredrag. [International Aspects on the Problems of the Underdeveloped Countries. A lecture.] (Foredrag og diskusjonsinnlegg på Det Nordiske nasjonaløkonomiske møte i Oslo 15.—17. juni 1961. Oslo 1962, pp. 15—35.)

365 Monetary Equilibrium. New York, A. M. Kelley, ca. 1962, XII, 214 pp. (Reprints of Economic Classics.) [Cf. 91a—d.]
Later repr.

366 Negrerna i framtidens Amerika. [The Negroes in the US of the Future.] (Vi 49 (1962) : 36, pp. 10—11, 42.)
Swedish abstract of a lecture at Howard University, Washington, D.C. [Cf. 358.]

367 Negro Problem: A Prognosis. (New Republic 147 (1962): July 9, pp. 11—12.)

368 I paesi del benessere e gli altri. La pianificazione negli stati di benessere e le sue implicazioni internazionali. [Orig. title:] Beyond the Welfare State. Trad. di Maria Grazia Bandini. Milano, Feltrinelli, 1962, 268 pp. (Saggi di economia e scienze sociali 6.) [Cf. 323e.]

369 Progress on the Road to Negro Integration. (AFL-CIO Free Trade Union News 17 (1962): 10, p. 8.)
Excerpts from an address on the occasion of the 94th Annual Commencement at Howard University, Washington, D. C. [Cf. 354, 358.]

370 Solidaridad o desintegración. Tendencias actuales de las relaciones económicas internacionales en el mundo no soviético. [Orig. title:] An International Economy. Problems and Prospects. Trad. de Salvador Echavarría y Enrique González Pedrero. 2ª ed. México & Buenos Aires, Fondo de cultura económica, 1962, 455 pp. [Cf. 246b.]

371 Våra affärer med u-länderna. 1—2. [Our Economic Relations with the Underdeveloped Countries.] (Tiden 54 (1962): pp. 12—24, 81—92.)

372a+* Vi och Västeuropa. Uppfordran till eftertanke och debatt. [We and Western Europe. Challenge to Reflection and Discussion.] [With] Tord Ekström & Roland Pålsson. Stockholm, Rabén & Sjögren, 1962, 164 pp. [Cf. 828.]
2nd and 3rd ed. same year.

372b Translation.
[Russian:] Švecija i zapadnaja Evropa. Moskva 1964. (434)

373 * Vi og Vesteuropa. [We and Western Europe.] (9 om de seks. 9 kritiske indlæg om de seks. København 1962, pp. 112—134.) [Cf. 372a.]

374¹ [Foreword to:] Nair, Kusum: De indiska byarna — rörelse i stagnation. [Orig. title: Blossoms in the Dust. Övers. av [Transl. by]: John O. Ericsson.] Stockholm 1962, pp. 7—11. [Cf. 347.]

374² Byråkrati och demokrati. [Bureaucracy and Democracy.] (Stockholms-Tidningen 7/10 1962.) [Cf. 375.]
Polemics with Wilhelm Paues about the Constitution of the West-European Community.

375 En byråkrats maktdrömmar. [A Bureaucrat's Dreams of Power.] (Stockholms-Tidningen 8/10 1962.) [Cf. 374.]
Continued polemics with Wilhelm Paues.

376 "Debatten måste bli offentlig." Gunnar Myrdal tar på nytt upp frågan om EEC. [The Debate Must Become Public. Gunnar Myrdal Resumes the Question of EEC.] (Stockholms-Tidningen 4/10 1962.) [Cf. 374—375, 377.]

377 Information till folket, inte bara till ett fåtal. [Information to the People in General, not Only to a Few.] (Stockholms-Tidningen 13/10 1962.) [Cf. 376.]
Reply to the Minister of Commerce Gunnar Lange in regard of his book "Vi och Västeuropa" and the principle of publicity.

378 'Integration' in Focus. (Justice 1/7 1962.)
Excerpts from Commencement Address at Howard University, Washington, D. C., June 8, 1962. [Cf. 354, 358, 388.]

379 Tal på Skansen vid invigningen av Stockholms FN-förenings utställning om FN den 24/10 1962. [Speech at Skansen, Stockholm, at the Opening of the Exhibition of the Stockholm UN Society, October 24, 1962.] (Stockholms-Tidningen 25/10 1962.)

380 Förnuft på väg att segra. [Reason on the Way to Be Victorious.] (Aftonbladet 3/10 1962.)
On account of riots in Mississippi. — Interview by Olle Tolgraven.

381 * Humanistprofessorer talar ut. Humanistöverskottet överdrivet. [Med uttalanden av ... Gunnar Myrdal.] [Humanist Professors Speak out. The Surplus of Humanists Exaggerated ...] (Gaudeamus 39 (1962): 11, p. 7.)
Interview.

382 Myrdal Terms U. S. 'Stagnant'; Urges Wide Economic Reform. (The New York Times 22/7 1962.)
Interview in Stockholm by Werner Wiskari.

383 Stormen var väntad. Högern vulkan under Europaytan. [The Storm Was Expected. The Conservatives a Volcano under the European Surface.] (Stockholms-Tidningen 4/9 1962.)
Interview by Sven O. Andersson.

1963

384 Amerikas väg — en uppfordran till överflödssamhället. [Orig. title:] Challenge to Affluence. Övers. [Transl.]: Hans

Granqvist & Ulrich Herz. Stockholm, Rabén & Sjögren, 1963, 210 pp. (Skrifter utg. av Utrikespolitiska Institutet.) [Cf. 387c.]
2nd ed. same year.

385 Beyond the Welfare State. (West and non-West. New Perspectives. An Anthology. Ed. by Vera Micheles Dean and Harry D. Harootunian. New York 1963, pp. 502—517.)
Excerpt from Beyond the Welfare State. (322)

386+ Challenge to Affluence. New York, Pantheon Books, 1963, 173 pp. [Cf. 387a, 395.]
Amended and enl. version of three McEnervey lectures at the University of California at Berkeley, in April, 1963.
With Appendix: Commencement Address at the 94th Commencement, Howard University, Washington, D. C., June 8, 1962, pp. 163 —172. [Cf. 358.]—Several repr.

387a — London, Victor Gollancz, 1963, 160 pp. [Cf. 386.]
Repr. 1974.

387b — Rev. and expanded ed. New York 1965. (455)

387c Translations.
[Danish:] Amerikas vej . . . Glostrup 1964. (411)
[Dutch:] Uitdaging aan de welvaart. Rotterdam 1965. (479)
[Finnish:] Ongelmien Yhdysvallat. Helsinki 1964. (423)
[Japanese:] Yutakasa he no chōsen. Tōkyō 1964. (441)
[Korean:] P'ungyo-eŭi chojaeng. Seoul 1974. (A36)
[Spanish:] El reto a la sociedad opulenta. México & Buenos Aires 1964. (431a—b)
[Swedish:] Amerikas väg . . . Stockholm 1963. (384)

388 Commencement Address. (386: Challenge to Affluence, pp. 163—172.) [Identical with 358.]
Commencement Address at the 94th Commencement, Howard University, Washington, D. C., June 8, 1962.

389 Cumulative Causation and Economic Planning. [Selections from . . . Rich Lands and Poor.] (History of Economic Thought. A Book of Readings. 2nd ed. [rev. and enl.]. Ed. by K. William Kapp & Lore L. Kapp. New York 1963, pp. 417—434.) [Cf. 265.]

390 Economic Theory and Under-Developed Regions. London, Methuen, 1963, 168 pp. (University Paperbacks 66.) [Cf. 255c.]

391[1] El estado del futuro. [Orig. title:] Beyond the Welfare State. Trad. de Florentino M. Torner. 2ª ed. México & Buenos Aires, Fondo de cultura económica, 1963, 295 pp. (Tiempo presente 25.) [Cf. 331b.]

391[2+] Food for Increasing Millions. (World Agriculture 12 (1963): 2/3, pp. 35—42.) [Cf. 462.]
Address at the World Food Congress, Washington, D. C., in June, 1963.

392 Fukushi kokka wo koete. Fukushi kokka deno keizai keikaku to sono kokusaiteki imi kanren. [Japanese transl. of: Beyond the Welfare State. Economic Planning in the Welfare States and Its International Implications.] Chief of compilation: Kazuo Kitagawa. Joint transl.: Itsuo Kawamura and Yoshio Matsunaga. Tōkyō, Diamond Inc., 1963, 285 pp. [Cf. 323e, 748.]

393 Getting America Moving. (New Republic 148 (1963): January 26, pp. 15—20.)
Excerpt from an address.

394 Gustav Cassel in memoriam (1866—1945). [Transl. by Göran Ohlin.] (Bulletin of the Oxford University Institute of Statistics 25 (1963): 1, pp. 1—10.) [Cf. 155.]

395 It's Time to Face the Future. (Look 27 (1963): November 19, p. 96 & passim.)
Excerpts from Challenge to Affluence. (387)

396 Kennedy borta. [Kennedy dead.] (Vi 50 (1963): 48, p. 14.)

397 Monetary Equilibrium. London, Cass, 1963, 214 pp. [Cf. 91a–d.]

398 Planifier pour développer. De l'état-providence au monde-providence. [Orig. title:] Beyond the Welfare State. Trad. par René Baretje. Paris, Editions ouvrières ..., 1963, 261 pp. (Économie et civilisation 7.) [Cf. 323e.]

53

399 Das politische Element in der nationalökonomischen Doktrinbildung. [Orig. title: Vetenskap och politik i nationalekonomien.] Mit einem Nachwort von Paul Streeten. Übers. ... an Hand der englischen Ausg. durch M. Schüler bearb. Hannover, Verlag für Literatur und Zeitgeschehen, 1963, 210 pp. (Schriftenreihe der Forschungsstelle der Friedrich-Ebert-Stiftung. A. Sozialwissenschaftliche Schriften.) [Cf. 11, 228, 715.]

400 The Role of Government in the Economy. (Challenges to Democracy. The Next Ten Years. Ed. by Edward Reed. New York & London 1963, pp. 9—30.)

401 Tax Less, Spend More — That's What Myrdal Advises. (U. S. News & World Report 55 (1963): December 16, p. 26.)
Summary of an address, December, 1963.

402 De toekomst van de welvaartsstaat. Met een ten geleide van J. Tinbergen ... [Orig. title:] Beyond the Welfare State. Nederlands van Pieter H. W. C. Rommers. Amsterdam, De Arbeiderspers, 1963, 270 pp. [Cf. 323e.]

403 The Widening Income Gap. (International Development Review 5 (1963): 3, pp. 3—6.)
This article is condensed from the author's address at the World Food Congress in Washington, in June, 1963. [Cf. 462.]

---

404 Förhållandet stat — industri. [The Relations between State and Industry.] (Stockholms-Tidningen 29/8 1963.)
Summary of a discourse in Stockholm, 1946.

405 Myten om överflödets samhälle. [The Myth of a Society of Affluence.] (Stockholms-Tidningen 25/1 1963.)

406 Staten och ekonomin. USA:s ekonomiska stagnation. [State and Economy. The Economic Stagnation of the US.] [1—2.] (Stockholms-Tidningen 23/1, 15/2 1963.)

407 Intermarriage and the Race Problem. See 409.

408 Tingsten ljuger väl inte men han har tagit miste. [Tingsten Doesn't Lie, I Suppose, but He Is Mistaken.] (Stockholms-Tidningen 19/8 1963.)

Refers to Professor Herbert Tingsten's pronouncement concerning the commercial treaty in 1946 between Sweden and the Soviet Union. — Interview by Gunnar Palin.

409 "You Can't Change Social Situation by Laws." Intermarriage and the Race Problem . . . (U. S. News & World Report 55: November 18, 1963, pp. 84—86.)

Interview in Stockholm, 1963.

1964

410 An American Dilemma. With the assistance of Richard Sterner and Arnold Rose. [With a new Preface by the author and a review of recent events by Arnold Rose.] Vol. 1—2. New York, Toronto & London, McGraw-Hill. (McGraw-Hill Paperbacks.) [Cf. 127c.]

1. The Negro in a White Nation. 1964, pp. I—LXXXIII, 1—520, LXXXIV—CCXXXIX. — 2. The Negro Social Structure. 1964, pp. I—XI, 521—1330.

"This edition reproduces the one-volume Twentieth Anniversary Edition."

411 Amerikas vej — en advarsel til overflodssamfundet. [Orig. title:] Challenge to Affluence. Overs. fra svensk [Transl. from Swedish] efter "Amerikas väg" af Lis Thorbjørnsen. Glostrup, Det Danske Forlag, 1964, 192 pp. [Cf. 387c.]

412 The Conditions of Economic Integration. (Development and Society. The Dynamics of Economic Change. Ed. by David E. Novack and Robert Lekachman. New York 1964, pp. 313—326.)

2nd pr. same year.

413 A Critical Appraisal of the Concept and Theory of Underemployment. (Essays on Econometrics and Planning Presented to Professor P. C. Mahalanobis . . . Oxford . . . Calcutta 1964, pp. 183—204.)

"This article is a draft of a methodological appendix in a book on South Asian development problems [Asian Drama (637)] on which the author is working."

414 [Diskussionsinlägg i anslutning till C. T. Saunders' föredrag Can Britain Escape from Her Balance of Payment Difficulties?] [Contribution to the debate in connection with C. T. Saunders's lecture ...] (Nationalekonomiska Föreningens Förhandlingar 1964, pp. 126—128.)
Meeting of the Society of Political Economy (Stockholm), December 7, 1964.

415 Framtidsutsikter. 1: Historien är människors verk. — 2: Om bara den politiska viljan fanns ... [Future Prospects. 1: History Is the Work of Men. — 2: If There Only Were a Political Will ...] (Vi 51 (1964): 38, p. 12; 39, p. 28.)
Swedish transl. of a speech at the Centennial Jubilee of Swarthmore College, Pennsylvania.

416 An International Economy. Problems and Prospects. New York/London, Harper & Brothers; Tokyo, Weatherhill, 1964, XIV, 381 pp. (A Harper International Student Reprint.) [Cf. 244b.]

417 International Inequalities. (Politics and Geographic Relationships... [Ed. by] W. A. Douglas Jackson. Englewood Cliffs, N. J., 1964, pp. 281—291.)
Repr. of Economic Theory and Under-Developed Regions. Chapter 5. (255a)

418 * Liberalism and the Negro. A Round-Table Discussion [between] James Baldwin, Nathan Glazer, Sidney Hook, Gunnar Myrdal [and Norman Podhoretz]. (Commentary 37 (1964): 3, pp. 25—42.) [Cf. 510.]

419 The Matrix. (Poverty in Plenty. Ed. by George H. Dunne ... New York 1964, pp. 118—142.)
Address given at the 175th Anniversary Conference on "Poverty-in-Plenty: The Poor in Our Affluent Society", held on January 23, 1964, in Gaston Hall, Georgetown University, Washington, D. C.

420 National State Policies in Underdeveloped Countries. (Politics and Geographic Relationships ... [Ed. by] W. A. Douglas Jackson. Englewood Cliffs, N. J., 1964, pp. 309—317.) [Cf. 260.]

421a al-Naẓarīyah al-iqtiṣādīyah wa-al-duwal al-nāmīyah. [Arabian transl. by 'Ibrāhīm al-Shaykh of Economic Theory and Under-Developed Regions.] al-Qāhirah, Dār al-Qawmīyah, 1964, 131 pp. [Cf. 255e.]

421b — al-Qāhirah 1967. (576)

422+ The Need of a Critical View and a Reorientation of Our Theoretical Approaches in Regard to the Problems of Underdeveloped Countries. (Entwicklungstheorie und Entwicklungspolitik. Gerhard Mackenroth zum Gedächtnis ... Tübingen 1964, pp. 507—530.)

423 Ongelmien Yhdysvallat. [Problematic USA.] [Orig. title:] Challenge to Affluence. Suomentanut [Transl. to the Finnish by] Raimo Malm. Helsinki, Aalto, 1964, 207 pp. [Cf. 387c.]

424 Överflödssamhällets problematik. [Problematics of the Society of Affluence.] (Vårt ekonomiska läge 1964, pp. 27—49.)
A somewhat enlarged text of a lecture at the Conference of The Swedish Savings Banks' Central Organization for Publicity and Propaganda, Stockholm, 27 February, 1964.

425 Planning in the Underdeveloped Countries. [Selection from Beyond the Welfare State, 1960.] (Economic Development. Evolution or Revolution? Ed. ... by Laura Randall. Boston 1964, pp. 106—111.) [Cf. 322.]

426 The Principle of Cumulation. With the assistance of Richard Sterner and Arnold Rose. (Social Change. Sources, Patterns, and Consequences. Ed. by Amitai and Eva Etzioni. New York & London 1964, pp. 455—458.) [Cf. 289.]
An American Dilemma. Appendix 3. A Methodological Note on the Principle of Cumulation, pp. 1065—1070. (127a)

427 Priorities in the Development Efforts of Underdeveloped Countries and Their Trade and Financial Relations with Rich Countries. Roma 1964, 8 pp. [Cf. 428—429, 762.]
Paper presented before the Società italiana per l'Organizzazione internazionale ..., March 18, 1964.

428 Priority in Development Efforts of Underdeveloped Countries. (Afro-Asian and World Affairs 1964.) [Cf. 427.]

429 Das Problem der Prioritäten in der Entwicklungspolitik. Aufgaben und Ansprüche der unterentwickelten Länder. [Orig. title: Priorities in the Development Efforts of Underdeveloped Countries . . .] [Trad. by John Oldenbourg.] (Europa-Archiv, Folge 19. 1964, pp. 727—738.) [Cf. 427.]

430 Problemet Sverige hjälper. [The Problem of Swedish Assistance.] (437a: Vår onda värld, pp. 124—170.) [Identical with 341.]

431a El reto a la sociedad opulenta. [Orig. title:] Challenge to Affluence. Trad. de Carlos Gerhard. México & Buenos Aires, Fondo de cultura económica, 1964, 222 pp. (Tiempo presente 53.) [Cf. 387c.]

431b — 2ª ed. México & Buenos Aires 1966. [Cf. 521.]

432⁺ The Role of Science and Technology in the Development of Underdeveloped Countries in South Asia. (The Emerging World. Jawaharlal Nehru memorial vol. New York 1964, pp. 119—135.)

433 Scelte economiche nei paesi sottosviluppati. [Transl. from the English orig. Economic Development in the Backward Countries.] (La Comunità Internazionale 19 (1964): 2, pp. 3—13.) [Cf. 563.]

434 * Svecija i zapadnaja Evropa. [Orig. title:] Vi och Västeuropa. [By] G. Mjurdal' [Gunnar Myrdal], R.Pol'sson [Roland Pålsson], & T. Ekstrem [Tord Ekström]. Perevod so švedskogo V. S. Komentaevskogo . . . Moskva, Progress, 1964, 172 pp. (Dlja naučnych bibliotek.) [Cf. 372b.]

435 Teoría económica y regiones subdesarrolladas. [Orig. title:] Economic Theory and Under-Developed Regions. Trad. de Ernesto Cuesta y Óscar Soberón. 2ª ed. México & Buenos Aires, Fondo de cultura económica, 1964, 189 pp. [Cf. 255e, 319.]

436   The Urgent Need for Scientific Breakthroughs if Great Misery Shall not be the Destiny of Underdeveloped Countries. (Global Impacts of Applied Microbiology. Ed.: Mortimer P. Starr. Stockholm ..., New York ... 1964, pp. 50—58.)

437a+¡Vår onda värld. [Our Evil World.] Övers. från delvis engelska manuskript av [Transl. from partly English ms. by] Ulrich Herz. Stockholm, Rabén & Sjögren, 1964, 217 pp. (Skrifter utg. av Utrikespolitiska Institutet.) [Cf. 486.]

437b   Translation.
       [Norwegian:] Vår truede verden. Oslo 1965. (486)

438   The War on Poverty. (The New Republic, February 8, 1964, pp. 121—127.) [Cf. 489, 831.]

439   The Worldwide Emancipation of Underdeveloped Nations. (Assuring Freedom to the Free. A Century of Emancipation in the USA. Arnold M. Rose, ed. Detroit 1964, pp. 97—118.) [Cf. 440.]
       Lecture, in 1963, at Wayne State University in honor of the one hundreth anniversary of the Emancipation Proclamation.

440   The Worldwide Emancipation of Underdeveloped Nations. (Phi Delta Kappan 45 (1964), pp. 413—417.)
       The article is a modification of a paper the author delivered at Wayne State University, in 1963. [Cf. 439.]

441   Yutakasa he no chōsen. [Japanese transl. of: Challenge to Affluence.] [Transl. by] Keiji Ohara and Yutaka Ikeda. Tōkyō, Takeuchi Shoten, 1964, 257 pp. [Cf. 387c.]

———

442   Amerikas betalningsbekymmer. [The Payment Difficulties of the US.] (Stockholms-Tidningen 20/11 1964.)
       Main part of an address at the Annual Conference of the American Chamber of Commerce in London, 1964. [Cf. 443.]

443 "Bitter brittisk medicin — men nöden har ingen lag."
[Bitter British Medicine — But Necessity Knows No Law.]
(Stockholms-Tidningen 19/11 1964.)
Introductory part of an address at the Annual Conference of the American
Chamber of Commerce in London, 1964. [Cf. 442.]

444 Expansion räcker ej! [Expansion Is Not Enough!] (Stockholms-Tidningen 21/4 1964.)
The author speaks of the US.

445 Industrialisering ingen mirakelmedicin. [Industrialization —
No Magic Medicine.] (Stockholms-Tidningen 31/3 1964.)

446 De rika länderna måste praktisera en handelspolitisk dubbel-
moral. [The Rich Countries Must Practise Doubleness in
Regard to Commercial Policy.] (Stockholms-Tidningen 1/4
1964.)

447 Unemployment in the United States from a Swedish Per-
spective. Colloquy with Gunnar Myrdal. (Lessons from
Foreign Labor Market Policies. Washington 1964, pp.
1471—1495.) (Selected Readings in Employment and
Manpower. Subcommittee on Employment and Manpower
of the Committee on Labor and Public Welfare, U.S.
Senate. 4.)
Interview.

1965

448 Address on 'The Significance for Agricultural Planning in
Underdeveloped Countries of the Population Development'.
(Rural Planning in Developing Countries. Report on the
Second Rehovoth Conference, Israel, August, 1963. General
ed. Raanan Weitz. London 1965, pp. 13—14, 285—287.)
Address at the Opening Session of the Rehovoth Conference on Com-
prehensive Planning of Agriculture ... at the Weizmann Institute of
Science, Rehovoth, Israel, August 19, 1963.

449 Alimentos para más millones bocas. [Orig. title: Food for
increasing millions.] (Informe del Congreso mundial de la
alimentación, Wáshington, D. C., 4—18 junio 1963. Vol. 2.
Roma 1965, pp. 18—28.) [Cf. 462.]

450 August 1964. (387: Challenge to Affluence . . . Postscript, pp. 150—165.) [Cf. 455.]

451 Behovet av protester. [The Need of Protests.] (Veckans Affärer 7 sept. 1965, p. 66.)

452 Beneath the Riches. A Social Quickening to the Problem of Poverty. (The Financial Times, April 12, 1965, pp. 13—14.)

453 Beyond the Welfare State. Economic Planning and Its International Implications. 4th pr. New Haven & London, Yale University Press, 1965, XIV, 287 pp. (Yale Paperbounds 94.) [Cf. 323b.]
Same text as 454, only title slightly different.

454 Beyond the Welfare State. Economic Planning in the Welfare States and Its International Implications. London, Methuen, 1965, 214 pp. (University Paperbacks 134.) [Cf. 323c, 453.]

455 Challenge to Affluence. Rev. and expanded ed. [With Postscript: August 1964, and Appendices. New York, Vintage, 1965, 183 pp. [Cf. 387b, 450, 456.]

456 Commencement Address, Lincoln University, June 7th, 1964. (455: Challenge to Affluence, pp. 177—183.)

458 Den dåraktiga utrikespolitiken. [Orig. title: Inherent Imperfections in Foreign Policy.] 1: Samlade kunskaper tas inte i bruk. [Collective Knowledge Is Not Made Use of.] — 2: Offer för egen propaganda. [Victim of One's Own Propaganda.] (Vi 52 (1965): 34, pp. 12—13, 34—35; 35, pp. 14—15, 36.) [Cf. 465, 620, 646.]

459 Economic Growth and Economic Policy in the United States. ([Svenska Handelsbankens] Index. [English ed.] 40 (1965): 3. Suppl., 12 pp. — [Swedish ed.] 40 (1965): 4. Suppl., 12 pp.) [Cf. 476.]

460 The Emergence of an "Under-Class" in America. (Economic Issues and Policies. Readings in Introductory Economics. [Condensed from Challenge to Affluence.] Ed. by Arthur L.

Grey, Jr., and John E. Elliott. 2nd [rev.] ed. New York . . .
1965, pp. 360—365.) [Identical with 700.]

461 Farmare i nyckelroll. [Farmers in a key-position.] (Vi 52
(1965): 19, pp. 24—26.)
Swedish transl. of a speech at the Congress of the American Agricultural
Association in Chicago, 1965.

462 Food for Increasing Millions. (Report of the World Food
Congress, Washington, D. C., 4 to 18 June, 1963. Vol. 2.
Rome 1965, pp. 17—26.) [Cf. 391², 403, 449, 471.]

463 The Future University. (484: The University in the American
Future, pp. 95—111.)

464 Gustav Cassel 1866—1945. (Lebensbilder grosser National-
ökonomen. Einführung in die Geschichte der politischen
Ökonomie. Hrsg. von Horst Claus Recktenwald. Köln &
Berlin 1965, pp. 487—498.) [Cf. 155.]
German transl. of 226.

465 Inherent Imperfections in Foreign Policy. (Washington
University Magazine, Summer 1965, pp. 21—24.) [Cf. 458,
533, 616, 620, 646, 932.]
The Fifth Annual Lecture of the Theresa M. Loeb Memorial Lectures,
St. Louis, Missouri, April 20, 1965.

466 Jobs, Food, and People. Why Agricultural Progress is the
Cornerstone of Economic Growth. [With a Summary in
French: Travail, Nourriture et Population: Pourquoi le
Progrès Agricole est-il la Clef de la Croissance Economique.]
(International Development Review 7: 2. June 1965, pp.
2—6.)
A slightly condensed version of the author's address on the opening day
of the SID Seventh World Conference in Washington last March [1965].

467 Liberty and Equality. (The Economics of Poverty. An
American Paradox. Ed. by Burton A. Weisbrod. Englewood
Cliffs, N. J., 1965, pp. 171—178.)

468 A Look at the Western Economics. (Anglo American Trade
News, January 1965.)

469 Monetary Equilibrium. New York, A. M. Kelley, 1965, XI, 214 pp. (Reprints of Economic Classics.) [Cf. 91a—d.]

470 Mot industriellt byggeri. [Towards Industrialised Building.] (Teknisk Tidskrift 95 (1965), pp. 1297—98.)
Report of the author's Opening Address, "Needs versus Capacity", on August 23, 1965, at the CIB Congress in Copenhagen. [Cf. 515.]

471 Nourrir les multitudes qui montent. [Orig. title: Food for Increasing Millions.] (Rapport du Congrès mondial de l'alimentation, Washington, D. C., 4—18 juin, 1963. Vol. 2. Rome 1965, pp. 21—31.) [Cf. 462.]

472 Perspectives de la planificació. [Orig. title:] Beyond the Welfare State. Trad. [catalana] de Mireia Bofill. Barcelona, Edicións 62, 1965, 310 pp. (Col·lecció a l'abast 28.) [Cf. 323e.]

473 The Principle of Cumulation. (Minority Problems. A Textbook of Readings in Intergroup Relations. Ed. by Arnold M. Rose and Caroline B. Rose. New York 1965, pp. 373—383.) [Cf. 289.]

474 Racial Inequality and the American Creed. [. . . from An American Dilemma. . . . Vol. 1—2. New York 1944, pp. XLI—XLII, 3—4, 6, 13—14, 17—19, 21—23; pp. 1021—1022 . . .] (The State of the Union. Commentaries on American Democracy. [Ed. by] Robert B. Dishman. New York 1965, pp. 405—411.) [Cf. 127a.]

475 A Summing Up. (Poverty in America. Ed. by Margaret S. Gordon. San Francisco 1965, pp. 431—444.)
Concluding Address at a National Conference held at the University of California, Berkeley, February 26—28, 1965.

476 Sviluppo economico e politica economica negli USA da Index, rivista economica della Svenska Handelsbanken. (Mondo economico 20 (1965): 50, pp. 17—24.) [Cf. 459.]

477 Tekniska möjligheter väntar på att bli utnyttjade. [Technical Potentialities Waiting to Be Exploited.] (Byggnadsindustrin 35 (1965), p. 1302.)
Extract from the author's Opening Address, "Needs versus Capacity", on August 23, 1965, at the CIB Congress in Copenhagen. [Cf. 515.]

478 Teoria econômica e regiões subdesenvolvidas. [Orig. title: Economic Theory and Under-Developed Regions.] Rio de Janeiro, Saga, 1965, 240 pp. [Cf. 255e, 327.]

479 Uitdaging aan de welvaart. [Orig. title:] Challenge to Affluence. Vertaald uit het Amerikans van P. H. W. C. Rommers. Rotterdam, Universitaire Pers Rotterdam, 1965, VIII, 168 pp. (U. P. R. Paperbacks 7.) [Cf. 387c.]

480 U-landshjälpen hotar gå mot en katastrof. [The Assistance of the Underdeveloped Countries Threatens to Become a Disaster.] (Företagsekonomi 32 (44) (1965), pp. 280, 282.) Summary of a speech at the 7th World Conference of the Society for International Development, Washington, 1965. [Cf. 482.]

481 The Under Class in the Great Society. (Challenges and Choice. St. Louis Post-Dispatch. A special suppl. September 26, 1965, pp. 13—15.) [Cf. 528, 597, 740.]

482 Underutveckling ett jordbruksproblem. [Underdevelopment a Problem of Agriculture.] (Kooperatören 52 (1965), pp. 293—296.) Swedish transl. of a part of a speech at the 7th World Conference of the Society for International Development, in Washington, 1965. [Cf. 480.]

483 The United Nations, Agriculture, and the World Economic Revolution. (Journal of Farm Economics 47 (1965), pp. 889—899.) [Cf. 733, 802.] Adapted from an Address to the Latin American Conference on Food and Agriculture held in Viña del Mar, Chile, March 18, 1965, by the Food and Agriculture Organization of the United Nations.

484 * The University in the American Future. [With] Kenneth D. Benne, Charles Morris [&] Henry Steele Commager. Ed. by Thomas B. Stroup. Lexington, University of Kentucky Press, 1965, XI, 111 pp. [Myrdal's article: The Future University, pp. 95—111.] Based upon lectures given during the Conference on Higher Education, held at the University of Kentucky, in May, 1965, as a part of the celebration of the University's Centennial.

485 O valor em teoria social. [Portuguese transl. by Oracy Nogueira of Value in Social Theory.] São Paulo, Liv. Pioneira, ed. da Universidade, 1965, 326 pp. [Cf. 300b.]

486 Vår truede verden. [Our Evil World.] Overs. av [Transl. by] Bjørn Bjørnsen. Oslo, Pax, 1965, 145 pp. (Pax-bøkene 20.) [Cf. 437b.]
Norwegian transl. from Ulrich Herz' Swedish version of partly English manuscripts.

487 Världens livsmedelsförsörjning. [The Food Supply of the World.] (Nordisk Lantbruksekonomisk Tidskrift 15 (1965), pp. 76—78.)
Lecture at the General Assembly of the Central Council of the Nordic Farmers' Organizations, Malmö, July 20, 1965.

488 Villkor för Vietnamfred. Protokoll för den direktsända radiodebatten den 4 okt. 1965. [Conditions for Peace in Vietnam. Broadcast discussion . . .] Red.: Karl-Olov Nordelius. [Stockholm 1965], pp. 12—14, 26—28, 33—34, 37—39, 43—44. [Stencil.]

489 The War on Poverty. (New Perspectives on Poverty. Ed. by Arthur B. Shostak and William Gomberg. Englewood Cliffs, N. J., 1965, pp. 121—127.) [Cf. 489, 831.]

490 The Wealth of America. (Financial Times, April 13, 1965.)

491 Das Wertproblem in der Sozialwissenschaft. [Orig. title: Value in Social Theory.] Mit einer Einführung und einem Anhang von Paul Streeten. Die Übers. besorgten (mit Ausnahme der Kapitel 1, 10 und 11) Suzanne Reichstein und Manfred Schüler. Hannover, Verlag für Literatur und Zeitgeschehen, 1965, 275 pp. (Schriftenreihe des Forschungsinstituts der Friedrich-Ebert-Stiftung. A. Sozialwissenschaftliche Schriften.) [Cf. 300b.]
Several chapters previously printed.

492 Will We Prevent Mass Starvation? (Congressional Record. Senate, May 7, 1965, p. 9515. — The New Republic, April 24, 1965, pp. 14—15.)

493 With What Little Wisdom the World Is Ruled. (New York Times Magazine 1965: July 18, pp. 20—21 & passim.)

494   World Famine Ahead? Gunnar Myrdal's Warning. (U. S. News & World Report 58 (1965): March 29, p. 16.)
Excerpts from an address, March 15, 1965.

495+   The 1965 McDougall [Memorial] Lecture. (914: Essays and Lectures, pp. 11—26. — C 65/LIM/ Rev. 1, Rome 1965.) [Identical with 507.]
Address at the opening of the Thirteenth Conference of the Food and Agriculture Organization of the United Nations, Rome, 22nd November, 1965.

---

496   [Foreword to:] Clark, Kenneth B.: Dark Ghetto. Dilemmas of Social Power. New York, Evanston & London 1965, pp. IX—XI. [Cf. 536—537.]

497   [Foreword to:] Hansen, Alvin H.: The Dollar and the International Monetary System. New York . . . 1965, pp. IX—XII. [Cf. 498.]

498   [Foreword to:] Hansen, Alvin H.: Dollarn och det internationella betalningssystemet. [The Dollar and the International Monetary System.] Stockholm 1965, pp. 7—10. [Cf. 497.]

499   [Foreword to:] Poverty as a Public Issue. Ed. with an introd. by Ben. B. Seligman. New York & London 1965, pp. V—IX.

500   Gunnar Myrdal en Comercio Mundial. (Comercio Mundial 7 (1965): Noviembre/diciembre, pp. 123—125.)
Interview.

501   Hur går [statsminister] Erlanders tal ihop med världens utveckling? [How Does Prime Minister Erlander's Speech Agree with the Development of the World?] (Götheborgske Spionen 1965: 16, pp. 16—17.)
Interview by Åke Magnusson.

1966

502 The Economic Effects of Population Development. (Economic Development. Issues and Policies. P. S. Lokanathan Seventy-Second Birthday Commemoration Volume. [Ed. by D. H. Butani and Pritam Singh.] Bombay 1966, pp. 33—52.)

503 The Effects Toward Integration in Rich and Poor Countries. [Cf. 745[1].]
Lecture in Mexico City, October 3, 1966.

504 Los Estados Unidos y los esfuerzos de integración en Europa. [Orig. title: The United States and the Integration Endeavors in Europe.] (Integración 3 (1966): 33, pp. 8—10; 34, pp. 10—12.) [Cf. 529.]

505 Famine on the Doorstep. (Freedom from Hunger 7 (1966): 41, pp. 24—28.)

506 FAO: the Imperative of Altruism. (The Nation 1966: Dec. 19, pp. 666-670.)

507 The Impending Calamity. Can It Be Averted? (The McDougall Memorial Lecture to the Conference of the Food and Agricultural Organization of the United Nations, Rome, 22nd Nov., 1965. Doc. C65/LIM/3, 13 pp.) [Identical with 495. Cf. 534.]
Published by the Australian Section of the Women's International League for Peace and Freedom . . . January, 1966.

508 Die kommende Welt-Ernährungskrise vor der FAO. (Neue Wege 60 (1966), pp. 5—14.)
German translation of the principal arguments of a speech made at the FAO Conference in Rome, in November, 1965. [Cf. 495.]

509 Land Reform in Its Broader Economic and Social Setting. (Economic Planning 2 (1966): 3, pp. 5—10. — Report of the World Land Reform Conference, 1966. Annex 5, pp. 63—67.) [Cf. 586, 589, 765, 801, 937.]
Opening Address at the Second World Land Reform Conference, held at FAO Headquarters in Rome, June 20, 1966.

510 * Liberalism and the Negro. A Round-Table Discussion [between] James Baldwin, Nathan Glazer, Sidney Hook, Gunnar Myrdal, and Norman Podhoretz. (Racial and Ethnic Relations. Selected Readings. Ed. by Bernard E. Segal. New York 1966, pp. 459—492.) [Cf. 418.]

511 A Methodological Note on the Principle of Cumulation. (Racial and Ethnic Relations. Selected Readings. Ed. by Bernard E. Segal. New York 1966, pp. 26—33.) [Identical with 289. Cf. 140.]

512 Närmaste åren skrämmer mig. [The Next Few Years Frighten Me.] (Veckans Affärer 1966: 15/16, p. 54.)

513 National Planning for Healthy Cities: Two Challenges to Affluence. (Planning for a Nation of Cities. Ed. by Sam Bass Warner, Jr. Cambridge, Mass., & London 1966, pp. 3—22.)
Concluding Address at the Conference on Planning for the Quality of Urban Life, Washington University, St. Louis, Missouri, April 21—23, 1965.

514 The Need for More Intensive Planning. (Views of America. Under the general editorship of Alan F. Westin . . . New York . . . 1966, pp. 48—56.)

515 Needs Versus Capacity. (Towards Industrialised Building . . . Ed. by the International Council for Building Research, Studies and Documentation. Amsterdam, London & New York 1966, pp. 1—6.) [Cf. 470, 477.]
Opening Address at the Third CIB Congress, Copenhagen, August 23, 1965.

516 A Note on "Accounting Prices" and the Role of the Price Mechanism in Planning for Development. (Swedish Journal of Economics 68 (1966), pp. 135—147.)
"This is one of the methodological appendices to a book on the development problems in South Asia that will shortly appear" [= Asian Drama]. [Cf. 637—641.]

517   Note on Interest Rates in South Asian Countries. (Swedish Journal of Economics 68 (1966), pp. 219—233.)

518   Los obstáculos al desarrollo económico. (De economía 19 (1966), julio/sept., pp. 393—422.)

519   Paths of Development. (New Left Review, No. 36: March—April 1966, pp. 65—74.) [Cf. 813.]

520   Psychological Impediments to Effective International Co-operation. (Man and International Relations . . . [Ed. by] J. K. Zawodny. Vol. 2. San Francisco [1966], pp. 756—769.) [Cf. 223.]

521   El reto a la sociedad opulenta. [Orig. title:] Challenge to Affluence. Trad. de Carlos Gerhard. 2ª ed. México & Buenos Aires, Fondo de cultura económica, 1966, 222 pp. (Tiempo presente 53.) [Cf. 431b.]

522   Solidaridad o desintegración. Tendencias actuales de las relaciones económicas internacionales en el mundo no soviético. [Orig. title:] An International Economy. Problems and Prospects. Trad. de Salvador Echavarría y Enrique González Pedrero. 3ª ed. México & Buenos Aires, Fondo de cultura económica, 1966, 455 pp. [Cf. 246c.]

523   Svälten ett världshot. [Starvation a Menace to the Whole World.] (Vi 53 (1966): 2, pp. 16—17, 35.) [Continuation of 531.]
      Swedish abstract of a speech at the FAO Conference in Rome, 1965.

524   Teoria economica e paesi sottosviluppati. [Orig. title:] Economic Theory and Under-Developed Regions. Trad. di Elisa Marengo e Vincenzo Vitello. Milano 1966, Feltrinelli, 165 pp. (SC/10 2.) [Cf. 255e, 318.]

525   Ti'ūrī-ji iqtiṣādī va kišvarhā-ji kam-rušd. [Persian transl. of Economic Theory and Underdeveloped Regions.] [1st pr.] Tihrān 1344 [= 1966], 224 pp. [Cf. 255e, 822.]

526 Total isolering hotar USA. (532: 5)

527 Towards a New World Stability. From Beyond the Welfare State (New Haven 1960), pp. 238—244, 251—264. (America's Role in the World Economy. The Challenge to Orthodoxy. Ed. . . . by Douglas F. Dowd. Boston 1966, pp. 114—128.) [Cf. 322.]

528 Underklassen i Amerika. [Orig. title: The Under Class in the Great Society.] (Vi 53 (1966): 16, pp. 11—12; 17, pp. 7, 9.) [Cf. 481, 597.]

529 The United States and the Integration Endeavors in Europe. (The Annual Lecture in Social Sciences at the University of California, Los Angeles, May 4, 1966.) [Cf. 504.]

530 Il valore nella teoria sociale. [Orig. title:] Value in Social Theory. A cura di Paul Streeten. Trad. di Sandro Sarti. Torino, Giulio Einaudi, 1966, XLVI, 261 pp. (Nuova biblioteca scientifica Einaudi 11.) [Cf. 300b.]

531 Vår globala likgiltighet. [Our Global Indifference.] (Vi 53 (1966): 1, pp. 12—13, 37.] [Continuation see 523.]
Swedish abstract of a speech at the FAO Conference in Rome, 1965.

532+ The Vietnam War and the Pólitical and Moral Isolation of America. Address in Madison Square Garden, New York, 8 December, 1966. [A selection of the address or parts of it under various titles in alphabetical and chronological order.]
1 The Dirty War 1—2. (Patriot 26/12, 27/12, 1966.)
1. America's Isolation over Vietnam. — 2. U. S. Delusions and Vietnam's Future.
Excerpts.
2 Krigen i Vietnam. USA's politiske og moralske isolering. [1—2.] (Politiken 9/12, 10/12 1966.)
Danish transl.
3 The Political and Moral Isolation of America. (The Gazette and Daily, December 22, 1966.)
Excerpts.
4 Presidenten [Lyndon B. Johnson] fikk ikke beskjed! [The President Was Not Informed!] (Dagbladet 16/12 1966.) [Continuation of 532: 7.]
Norwegian transl.

5   Total isolering hotar USA. [The US in Danger to Be Completely Isolated.] (Vi 53 (1966): 50/51, pp. 76—77.)
Swedish transl.

6   USA och Vietnam-kriget. [The US and the Vietnam War.] (Värmlands Folkblad 9/12 1966.)
Swedish transl.

7   Vietnam isolerer USA. (Dagbladet 14/12 1966.) [Continued by 532: 4.]
Norwegian transl.

8   The Viet-Nam War 1—3. (Dawn, December 25, 27—28, 1966.)
1. Political, Moral Isolation of America. — 2. Conflict May Take Even Worse Turn. — 3. Superficial Knowledge of Asian Realities.

9   En farlig ledare. [A Dangerous Leader.] (Vi 54 (1967): 1, pp. 20—21.)
Swedish transl. of the 2nd part of the speech.

10   La guerre du Viet-nam et l'isolement moral et politique des Etats-Unis. (La Revue nouvelle 23 (1967): 45, pp. 410—418.)
French transl.

11   Der Krieg [in Vietnam], der nie erklärt wurde. (Die Weltbühne 22 (1967), pp. 522—525.)
German transl. of an excerpt.

12   Der Krieg in Vietnam und die politische und moralische Isolierung Amerikas. Übers. [Transl.]: Walter Hacker. (Arbeit und Wirtschaft 21 (1967): 1, pp. 2—9. — Toleranz, Verständigung, Friede, Nr. 5. 1967. pp. 1—13.)
German transl.

13   Krigen i Vietnam. USA's politiske og moralske isolering. (Dansk Udsyn 47 (1967), pp. 19—33.)
Danish transl.

14   Mihin menet, Amerikka? [Where Do You Go, America?] (Suomen kuvalehti 51 (1967): 5, pp. 24—25, 52.)
Finnish transl. of an excerpt.

15   Ne' prestigio ne' gloria. (L'Astrolabio 5 (1967): 3, pp. 27—31.)
Italian transl.

16   Der nichterklärte Krieg [in Vietnam]. (Express International 4 (1967): 41, p. 12.)
German transl.

17   Political and Moral Isolation of America. (Pax et Libertas 32 (1967), pp. 1—4.)

18 Show of Power in Vietnam only Turning US into a Lonely Giant. (The Guardian, January 6, 1967.)
Shortened version.

19 U rokovoj černy. [At the Fatal Line.] (Izvestija 8/1 1967.)
Russian transl. of an excerpt.

20 U. S. Politically, Morally Isolated. From Address to Sane Rally. (Sane World, January 1967, pp. 3, 5.)

21a USA och Vietnamkriget. [The US and the Vietnam War.] [1:] Total isolering hotar USA. [The US in Danger to Be Completely Isolated.] — [2:] En farlig ledare. [A Dangerous Leader.] Stockholm, Vietnampress, 1967, 13 pp.
Swedish transl.

21b — 2nd ed. Stockholm, Vietnampress, 1967, 14 pp.
With maps of Vietnam and observations by Stephen M. Young and David Shoup.

22 USA:s moraliska isolering. [The Moral Isolation of the US.] [Transl. by Olof Hoffsten.] (Dramatens Programblad 1966/67: 17, pp. 4—11.)
Swedish transl.

23 V'etnamskaja vojna i svjazannaja s nej političeskaja i moral'naja izoljacija Soedinennych Statov. (Mir nauki 1967: 3, pp. 3—10.)
Russian transl.

24 Vietnam: discorso agli americani. [Transl. by Mario Materassi.] (Il Ponte 23 (1967), pp. 324—337.)
Italian transl.

25 Vietnam — eine menschliche Tragödie. (Volksrecht 70 (1967): 14. Januar.)
German transl. of an excerpt.

26 Vietnam en de isolatie van Amerika. (Vrij Nederland 27 (1967): 22, p. 13.)
Dutch transl. of the 2nd part of the speech. [Cf. 532: 27.]

27 Vietnam en de politieke en morele isolatie van Amerika. (Vrij Nederland 27 (1967): 21, p. 11.
Dutch transl. of the 1st part of the speech. [Cf. 532: 26.]

28 Vietnam — una condanna per l'America. (Paese Sera. Ed. del mattino, 18 (1967): 17/1.)
Italian transl.

29 The Vietnam War and the Political and Moral Isolation of America. (Afro-Asian and World Affairs 4 (1967): 1,

pp. 1—12. — New University Thought 5 (1967): 3, pp. 3—12. — Scientific World 11 (1967): 3, pp. 5—10.)

30 Der Vietnamkrieg und die politisch-moralische Isolierung Amerikas. (Neue Wege 61 (1967): 1, pp. 10—13.) [Identical with 532: 31—32.]
German transl.

31 Der Vietnamkrieg und die politische und moralische Isolierung Amerikas. (Wissenschaftliche Welt 11 (1967): 3, pp. 4—11.) [Identical with 532: 30, 32.]
German transl.

32 Der Vietnamkrieg und die politische und moralische Isolierung der Vereinigten Staaten. (Gewerkschaftliche Monatshefte 18 (1967), pp. 65—74.) [Identical with 532: 30—31.]
German transl.

33 Wietnam a izolacja USA. (Świat 17 (1967): 4, pp. 6—7.)
Polish transl. of an excerpt.

34 Isolamento político e moral dos Estados Unidos. (Cadernos D[om] Quixote 7. Lisboa 1968, pp. 9—38.)
Portuguese transl.

35 Vietnamkriget och Förenta staternas politiska och moraliska isolering. (674: Utväg ur Vietnam? 1968, pp. 27, 29—48.)
Swedish transl.

36 Der Vietnamkrieg und die politische und moralische Isolierung Amerikas. (789: Aufsätze und Reden. 1971, pp. 53—69.)
German transl.

37 The Vietnam War and the Political and Moral Isolation of America. (914: Essays and Lectures. 1973, pp. 73—86.)

533 Von der Unvernunft in der Aussenpolitik. [Orig. title: Inherent Imperfections in Foreign Policy.] Übers. und Auswahl durch Ernst Schwarz. (Toleranz, Verständigung, Friede, Nr. 4. 1966, pp. 12—15.) [Cf. 465.]
Extract from the Swedish transl. in Vi. (458)

534 Die Welternährungsprobleme der nächsten Dekaden. [Orig. title: The Impending Calamity. Can It Be Averted?] (Aussenpolitik 17 (1966), pp. 142—152.) [Cf. 507.]

535 The World Is Heading for a Collision. (Man and Metal 43: 2. 1966, pp. 48—49, 52. — Unesco Courier 19 (1966): February, pp. 10—11.)
Conclusion of a lecture in November, 1965, in Rome under the auspices of FAO. — Transl. into several languages.

536 [Foreword to:] Clark, Kenneth B.: Ghetto noir. Harlem au microscope. Trad. par Yves Malartic. [Orig. title: Dark Ghetto . . .] Paris 1966, pp. 5—7. [Cf. 496.]

537 [Foreword to:] Clark, Kenneth B.: Det svarta ghettot. De amerikanska samhällsbyggarnas problem. Till svenska av Gunnar Barklund [Orig. title: Dark Ghetto . . .] Stockholm 1966, pp. 9—11. [Cf. 496.]

538 Can There Be Too Much of a Welfare State? 1—2. (Indian Express, May 13—14, 1966.)

539 The Dirty War 1—2. (532: 1)

540 Gustav Cassel. [To the 100th anniversary of his birth.] [Swedish text.] (Svenska Dagbladet 20/10 1966.) [Cf. 826.]

541 Krigen i Vietnam. USA's politiske og moralske isolering. (532: 2)

542 The Political and Moral Isolation of America. (532: 3)

543 Presidenten [Lyndon B. Johnson] fikk ikke beskjed! (532: 4)

545 Swedish Way to Happiness. (New York Times Sunday Magazine 1966: January 30, pp. 14—15, 17—18, 20—22.) [Cf. 547—548.]

546 USA och Vietnam-kriget. (532: 6)

547 Välfärden och hierarkierna. [Welfare and the Hierarchies.] (Svenska Dagbladet 6/2 1966.) [Cf. 545.]

548 Välfärdsstaten i blickpunkten. [The Welfare State in Focus.] (Svenska Dagbladet 30/1 1966.) [Cf. 545.]

549 Vietnam isolerer USA. (532: 7)

550 The Viet-Nam War 1—3. (532: 8)

552 De rike lands fremtid står og faller med u-landenes. Professor Gunnar Myrdal efterlyser menneskelig solidaritet. [The Future of the Rich Countries Stands and Falls with That of the Underdeveloped Countries. Prof. Myrdal Wants Human Solidarity.] (Aftenposten 26/3 1966.)
Interview with Gunnar Myrdal in Stockholm in March, 1966, by Jorunn Johnsen.

1967

553 Address. In Commemoration of the Twentieth Anniversary of the Economic Commission for Europe, April 12, 1967. [Sine loco] [1967], 29 pp. [Cf. 591, 673.]

554+ Address [at] ADA 20th Annual Convention, Shoreham Hotel, Washington, D. C. (Congressional Record — House, May 11, 1967, pp. 5388—5391.) [Cf. 581, 603.]

555 Adjustment of Economic Institutions in Contemporary America. The Trends of Changes Now Underway. (Institutional Adjustment. A Challenge to a Changing Economy ... Ed. by Carey C. Thompson. Austin & London 1967, pp. 69—84.)
Paper read at a Symposium sponsored by the Department of Economics of the University of Texas.

556 America and Vietnam. (606: 1)

557 An American Dilemma. (The Struggle for Racial Equality ... Sel. and ed. by Henry Steele Commager. New York 1967, pp. 1—3.) [Cf. 127a.]

558 Arme Länder werden immer ärmer. (Sozialistische Hefte 6 (1967), pp. 471—475.)

559 Beyond the Welfare State. Economic Planning and Its International Implications. New York, Toronto & London,

Bantam Books, 1967, XIII, 239 pp. (Bantam Matrix Editions.) [Cf. 323d.]

560+ Blir inflation oundviklig i en demokrati av den svenska typen? [Will Inflation Be Inevitable in a Democracy of the Swedish Type?] (Samhälle i omvandling. Stockholm 1967, pp. 127—152.)
The book dedicated to Tore Browaldh.

561 Chairman's Introduction. ([Symposium, London, 1966, on] Caste and Race. Comparative Approaches. A Ciba Foundation Volume. Ed. by Anthony de Reuck & Julie Knight. London 1967, pp. 1—4.)

562 Closing Address to the [Stockholm] World Conference on Vietnam [in July, 1967]. (606: 2)

563 Economic Development in the Backward Countries. (Dissent 1967: March—April, pp. 180—190.) [Cf. 433, 649.]
Paper originally presented before the Società italiana per l'Organizzazione internazionale.

564 An Economist's Vision of a Sane World. (Cahiers économiques et sociaux 5: 4. 1967, pp. 503—515.) [Cf. 650, 912.]
Lecture sponsored by the 1967 Exhibition in Montreal under the theme "Man and His World", May 29, 1967.

565 El elemento político en el desarrollo de la teoría económica. [Orig. title:] The Political Element in the Development of Economic Theory. Versión española de la 3ª ed. [= repr.] (1961) de José Díaz García. Madrid, Gredos, 1967, 242 pp. (Biblioteca de ciencias económicas 1. Teoría económica.) [Cf. 233.]

566 En farlig ledare. (532: 9)

567 * Før datamaskinene overtar. ([Orig. title:] The Triple Revolution.) Memorandum til USA's president [Lyndon B. Johnson] fra Gunnar Myrdal, Linus Pauling m. fl. Kommentar av Dave Dellinger ... Forord av Ole Wiig. [Before Computers Take Over. A Memorandum to the President of the U. S. from ... Comments by ... Preface by ... Red.

og overs. av [Ed. and publ. by] Johan Ludwig Mowinckel. Oslo, Pax, 1967, 75 pp. (Mini-Pax 14.)

568   La guerre du Viet-nam et l'isolement moral et politique des États-Unis. (532: 10)

569   Hvorfor handelen mellem Øst og Vest er så lille. [Why Trade between East and West is so Inconsiderable.] (Kontakt. Østeuropa 20 (1967): 8, pp. 18—21.) [Cf. 622.]

570   Keizai-gakusetsu to seijiteki yōso. [Rewritten Japanese transl. of the English transl. [The Political Element in the Development of Economic Theory] of Das politische Element in der nationalökonomischen Doktrinbildung.] [Transl. by] Yuzo Yamada and Ryuzo Sato. Tōkyō, Shunju Sha, 1967, 18, (6), 349, (13) pp. [Cf. 26, 102, 228a.]
2nd pr. 1970. — 3rd pr. 1975.

571   Der Krieg [in Vietnam], der nie erklärt wurde. (532: 11)

572   Der Krieg in Vietnam und die politische und moralische Isolierung Amerikas. (532: 12)

573   Krigen i Vietnam. USA's politiske og moralske isolering. (532: 13)

574[1]   En liten fotnot till historien. (Festskrift till Jacob Wallenberg. Stockholm 1967, pp. 587—590.)
Printed only in one copy.

574[2+]   Mihin menet, Amerikka? (532: 14)

575   Missionen arbetar utan svinn. [The Mission Works without a Loss.] (Vår kyrka 108 (1967): 25/26, pp. 10, 23.)
Contribution to a debate on assistance to underdeveloped countries.

576   al-Naẓarīyah al-iqtiṣādīyah wa-al-duwal al-nāmīyah. [Arabian transl. by 'Ibrāhīm al-Shaykh of Economic Theory and Under-Developed Regions.] al-Qāhirah, Dār al-Qawmīyah, 1967, 131 pp. [Cf. 421.]

577   Ne' prestigio ne' gloria. (532: 15)

578 Negerproblemets lösning — en fråga om de vitas moral. [The Solution of the Negro Issue — a Question of the Whites' Morals.] (Vi 54 (1967): 31/32, pp. 20—25.) [Cf. 587.]

579 Der nichterklärte Krieg [in Vietnam]. (532: 16)

580 Not Just Negroes. (Senior Scholastic 91 (1967): October 19, p. 13.)

581 "Om 15 år kan helvetet ha brutit lös." [Within 15 Years Hell May Have Broken Out.] (Vår kyrka 106 (1967): 34, pp. 13, 17.)
Swedish extract of a lecture in April, 1967, at the Annual Meeting of ADA. [Cf. 554.]

582 Planning in the Welfare State. (The Welfare State. Selected Essays. Ed. by Charles I. Schottland. New York, Evanston & London 1967, pp. 106—111.) (The Contemporary Essays Series.)

583 Planning the Future Society. Necessity and Difficulty. (Pax et Libertas 32 (1967), pp. 40—43.) [Cf. 661.]

584 Political and Moral Isolation of America. (532: 17)

585 Principles in Economic Research. (Economic Planning 3: 4. 1967, pp. 5—8.)
"Professor Myrdal's paper contains excerpts of the Prologue to his new great study 'Asian Drama' — to be published in the near future." [Cf. 637.]

586 Probleme der Landreform. Eine Lebensfrage der armen Länder. [Orig. title: Land Reform in Its Broader Economic and Social Setting.] (Sozialistische Hefte 6 (1967), pp. 563—566.) [Cf. 509.]

587 The Racial Crisis in Perspective. [With] Further Comments. (The Black American and the Press. Ed. by Jack Lyle. Los Angeles, Cal., 1967, pp. 5—15, 22—25.) [Cf. 578, 588, 809.]
Introductory lecture to a Symposium at the University of California, Los Angeles, May 24, 1967, and sponsored by the Department of Journalism.

588 Raskrisen i perspektiv. [The Racial Crisis in Perspective.] (Se 30 (1967): 31, pp. 23—24, 52. — Vi 54 (1967): 31/32, pp. 21—25.) [Cf. 587.]

589 La réforme agraire dans un contexte économique et social élargi. [Orig. title: Land Reform in Its Broader Economic and Social Setting.] (Notes et études documentaires, 27 novembre 1967. No 3439—3440, pp. 67—74.) [Cf. 509.]
Report from the World Land Reform Conference, Rome, 20 June—2 July, 1966. (Annexe 5.)

590 Relación entre la teoría social y la política social. [Orig. title: The Relation between Social Theory and Social Policy.] (Ciencias políticas y sociales 13 (1967): abril/junio, pp. 234—276.) [Cf. 230.]

591 Samarbetssträvanden mellan öst och väst i Europa. [Efforts of Cooperation between East and West in Europe.] (Världshorisont 21 (1967): 6, pp. 13—15, 17.)
From English translated summary of a lecture given in ECE, Geneva, on April 12, 1967. [Cf. 553.]

592 Slutanförande [vid Stockholmskonferensen om Vietnam 6—9 juli 1967]. (606: 3)

593 The State and the Individual. (The Welfare State. Selected Essays. Ed. by Charles I. Schottland. New York, Evanston & London 1967, pp. 214—221.) (The Contemporary Essays Series.)

594 Summons to Action. (The Victor Fund for the International Planned Parenthood Federation. Report 7. Fall 1967, 13—15.)

595 Sverige och världen. [Sweden and the World.] (Broderskap 39 (1967): 13, pp. 12—13. — Svensk Missionstidskrift 55 (1967), pp. 129—134.)
Speech at the Brotherhood Movement Congress in Skellefteå (Sweden), August 3—6, 1967.

596 The Theories of 'Stages of Growth'. (The Scandinavian Economic History Review 15 (1967): 1/2, pp. 1—12. [Offprint 1967, 12 pp.])

597 Underklassen i the Great Society. [Transl. into Swedish by Sigrid Åkerman.] [Orig. title: The Under Class in the Great Society.] (Konkret 1967: 2, pp. 51—54, 30.) [Cf. 481.] Another transl. than 528.

598 U. S. Politically, Morally Isolated. From Address to Sane Rally. (532: 20)

599 USA och Vietnamkriget. (532: 21a—b)

600 USA:s moraliska isolering. (532: 22)

601 *Vad är EEC värt? [What is the Value of the EEC?] Medverkande [Participants]: Axel Iveroth, Gunnar Myrdal, Gunnar Lange. Producent: Gustaf Olivecrona. (Prod.nr. 67/5806.) [Stencil.] Broadcast discussion.

602 Varför har socialvetenskaperna så litet inflytande på samhällsutvecklingen? [Why Do the Social Sciences Have so little Influence on the Development of Society?] (Människans villkor. En bok av vetenskapsmän för politiker red. av Karl-Erik Fichtelius. Stockholm 1967, pp. 157—166. (Nu! 3.) Also later editions.

603 Världens och Amerikas problem. [The Problems of the World and of America.] (Tiden 59 (1967), pp. 328—337.) Swedish transl. of the principal parts of a lecture in April, 1967, at the Annual Meeting of ADA. [Cf. 554.]

604 Det värsta som kan hända är en inbördes kamp mellan de fattiga. [Kommentarer till raskrisen.] [The Worst that Might Happen Is a Struggle between the Poor.] [Comments to the Race Crisis.] (Se 30 (1967): 31, pp. 23—24, 52.) [Cf. 587.]

605 V'etnamskaja vojna i svjazannaja s nej političeskaja i moral'naja izoljacija Soedinennych Statov. (532: 23)

606+ Vietnam — a Moral Problem for the Whole World. Closing Address at the Stockholm World Conference on Vietnam, July 6—9, 1967. [A selection of the address or parts of it under various titles in alphabetical and chronological order.]

1 America and Vietnam. (Transition 7: 33. Oct./Nov. 1967, pp. 14—18.)

2 Closing Address to the [Stockholm] World Conference on Vietnam [in July, 1967]. (Afro-Asian and World Affairs 4: 3. 1967, pp. 232—237.)

3 Slutanförande [vid Stockholmskonferensen om Vietnam 6—9 juli 1967]. (Vår Kyrka 108 (1967): 30, pp. 10—11, 16.)
Swedish transl. of an excerpt.

4 Vietnam — a Moral Problem for the Whole World. (Review of International Affairs 1967: 18, pp. 8—10.)
Excerpt.

5 Vietnam — ein moralisches Problem für die Welt. (Sozialistische Hefte 6 (1967), pp. 612—616.)
German transl.

6 Vietnam — en moralisk fråga för hela världen. [Stockholm 1967], 8 pp.
A folder with Swedish text based on the articles in the Dagens Nyheter and ed. by the Continuation Committee of the Stockholm Conference on Vietnam.

7 Vietnam — en moralisk fråga för hela världen. (Dagens Nyheter 26/7 1967.)
Swedish transl. of P. 1 of the Closing Address at the Stockholm World Conference on Vietnam.

8 Vietnam. En moralisk fråga för hela världen. (Kristet Forum 6. 1967, pp. 187—191.)
Swedish transl.

9 Vietnam, et moralsk spørsmål. (Dagbladet 10/8, 11/8 1967.)
Norwegian transl.

10 Vietnamkriget: Amerikas moraliska isolering. (Dagens Nyheter 27/7 1967.)
Swedish transl. of P. 2 of the Closing Address at the Stockholm World Conference on Vietnam.

11 Vietnam — ett moraliskt problem för hela världen. (674: Utväg ur Vietnam?, pp. 49, 51—64.)
Swedish transl.

12 Vietnam — ein moralisches Problem für die Welt. (789: Aufsätze und Reden, pp. 70—81.)
German transl.

607 Vietnam — a Moral Problem for the Whole World. (606: 4)

608 Vietnam: discorso agli americani. (532: 24)

609 Vietnam — ein moralisches Problem für die Welt. (606: 5)

610 Vietnam. En moralisk fråga för hela världen. (606: 8)

611 Vietnam — en moralisk fråga för hela världen. (606: 6)

612 The Vietnam War and the Political and Moral Isolation of America. (532: 29)

613 Der Vietnamkrieg und die politisch-moralische Isolierung Amerikas. (532: 30)

614 Der Vietnamkrieg und die politische und moralische Isolierung Amerikas. (532: 31)

615 Der Vietnamkrieg und die politische und moralische Isolierung der Vereinigten Staaten. (532: 32)

616 Vrozené vady zahraniční politiky. [Czech transl. of Inherent Imperfections in Foreign Policy.] (Mezinárodní politika 11 (1967), pp. 218—219.) [Cf. 465.]

617 Wietnam a izolacja USA. (532: 33)

———————

618 * Det gäller dig. En sektion om u-landsbistånd. [Artiklar av . . . Gunnar Myrdal . . .] [You Are the Addressee. A Section about Help to Underdeveloped Countries.] (Arbetet 21/10 1967, bilaga [appendix].)

619 Farget i USA. [The Negroes in USA.] (Dagbladet 27/7, 28/7 1967.)

620 Finns förnuft i utrikespolitiken? [Any Sense in Foreign Politics?] (Arbetet 7/2 1967. [Special number on Vietnam.]) [Cf. 465.]

621 Hva er galt med velferdsstaten? [What Is Wrong with the Welfare State?] [1—2.] (Dagbladet 13/2, 15/2 1967.) [Cf. 968.]

622[1] Öst-västhandeln i Europa. [East-West Trade Relations in Europe.] (Dagens Nyheter 24/9 1967.) [Cf. 569, 648, 729.]

622[2] Show of Power in Vietnam only Turning US into a Lonely Giant. (532: 18)

623 U rokovoj čerty. [At the Fatal Line.] (532: 19)

624 [Vietnam.] [Articles by ... Gunnar Myrdal ...] (Arbetet 7/2 1967, bilaga [appendix].)

625 Vietnam — eine menschliche Tragödie. (532: 25)

626 Vietnam en de isolatie van Amerika. (532: 26)

627 Vietnam en de politieke en morele isolatie van Amerika. (532: 27)

628 Vietnam — en moralisk fråga för hela världen. (606: 7)

629 Vietnam, et moralsk spørsmål. (606: 9)

630 Vietnam — una condanna per l'America. (532: 28)

631 Vietnamkriget: Amerikas moraliska isolering. (606: 10)

632 The American Dilemma 1967. (The Center Magazine 1: 1. October/November 1967, pp. 30—33.)
Interview by Donald McDonald.

633 Nationalekonomen som blev samhällskonflikternas kartläggare. [The Political Economist Who Mapped out the Social Conflicts ...] (Konkret 1967: 7/8, pp. 8—11, 13—15, 17, 19.) [Identical with 777.]
A Konkret Interview by Nordal Åkerman in October, 1967.

634 Profeten från Solvarbo. [The Prophet from Solvarbo.] (Röster i Radio-TV 1967: 4, pp. 18—19, 51.)
Interview by Annmari Lindh.

635 U. S. Crisis Worst Since Civil War. (The Dayton Daily News, November 12, 1967.)
Interview in Columbus, Ohio, by Dave Allbaugh.

1968

636 American Values and American Behavior. A Dilemma. [Abridgment of pp. XLV—XLIX, 1027—1031 of An American Dilemma. Vol. 1—2. New York & London 1944.] (Democracy, Pluralism, and the Social Studies. Readings and Commentary ... Ed. by James P. Shaver [&] Harold Berlak. Boston, Mass., ... 1968, pp. 86—96.) [Cf. 127a.]

637 Asian Drama. An Inquiry Into the Poverty of Nations. A Twentieth Century Fund Study. Foreword [by] August Heckscher. Principal assistants: William J. Barber, Altti Majava, Alva Myrdal, Paul P. Streeten, David Wightman, George W. Wilson. Vol. 1—3. New York, The Twentieth Century Fund, 1968, pp. I—XXX, 1—705; I—XVI, 707—1530; I—XVII, 1531—2284. [Cf. 638—643, 669, 680, 688, 707, 735, 739, 766, 787, 790, 796, 902, 992.]

638 — New York, Pantheon, 1968. [Cf. 637.]

639 — Harmondsworth, Penguin Books, 1968. (A Pelican Book.) [Cf. 637.]

640 — London, Allen Lane The Penguin Press, 1968. [Cf. 637.]

641a — Taipei 1968. [Cf. 637.]
Pirate edition.

641b [—] An Approach to the Asian Drama ... Selections ... New York 1970. (735)

641c — An Abridgment by Seth S. King ... New York 1971. (786)

641d — An Abridgement by Seth S. King ... London 1972. (848)

84

641e — An Abridgment by Seth S. King . . . New York 1972. (847)

641f Translations.
[French:] Le drame de l'Asie. [Condensed ed.] Paris 1976.
(1045)
[German:] Asiatisches Drama . . . in der Kurzfassung von
Seth S. King. Frankfurt am Main 1973. (900)
[Italian:] Saggio sulla povertà di undici paesi asiatici.
[Complete ed.] Milano 1971. (819)
[—] Il dramma dell'Asia. Ed. abbreviata . . . a cura di
Seth King. Milano 1973. (909²)
[Japanese:] Ajia no dorama. [. . . An Abridgment by Seth
S. King.] Tōkyō 1974. (981)
[Korean:] Asia-ŭi tŭrama. [Condensed ed.] Seoul 1976.
(1041)
[Norwegian:] Asiatisk drama. [Condensed ed.] Oslo 1969.
(698)
[Russian:] Sovremennye problemy "tret'ego mira". [Drama
Azii . . .] [Shortened ed.] Moskva 1972. (869)
[Spanish:] La pobreza de las naciones. Ed. abreviada a
cargo de Seth S. King. Barcelona 1974. (997²)
[Swedish:] Asiatiskt drama. [Condensed ed.] Stockholm
1968—70. (643, 699, 736)
[Urdu:] Aišian drāma. [Condensed ed.] Karachi 1975.
(1015²)

642 Asian Drama. (Nationalekonomiska Föreningens Förhand-
lingar 1968, pp. 41—72 [incl. discussion].)
Lecture at the meeting of the Society of Political Economy (Stockholm),
April 29, 1968.

643 Asiatiskt drama. En undersökning om nationernas fattigdom.
[Orig. title:] Asian Drama. An Inquiry into the Poverty of
Nations. [Förkortad utgåva.] [Shortened ed.] Stockholm,
Rabén & Sjögren, [Helsingfors, Söderström]. (Skrifter utg. av
Utrikespolitiska Institutet.) [Cf. 641 f.]
[1.] Politiska problem i Sydasien. [Political Problems in South Asia.]
Bemyndigad övers. av [Authorized transl. by] Roland Adlerberth. 1968,
VIII, 367 pp. — 2nd ed. same year. [Cf. 699, 736.]
Corresponds to P. 2 and 4: Chapter 16 of Asian Drama. (637)

644+ Bostadssociala preludier. [Preludes to a Housing Policy.]
(Bostadspolitik och samhällsplanering. [Hyllningsskrift till
Alf Johansson.] Stockholm 1968, pp. 9—14.)

646 Den dåraktiga utrikespolitiken. [Orig. title: Inherent Im-

perfections in Foreign Policy.] (674: Utväg ur Vietnam? pp. 9, 11—26.) [Cf. 458, 465.]

647 Development and Underdevelopment. (Reshaping the World Economy. Rich and Poor Countries. Ed. by J. A. Pincus. Englewood Cliffs 1968, pp. 85 91.) (A Spectrum Book 176.) [Cf. 240.]

648 East-West Economic Relations in Europe. (New Hungarian Quarterly 9: 29. 1968, pp. 27—37.) [Cf. 622¹.]
Paper read at the Budapest International Colloquium on Economic Integration and East-West Trade, September 10—14, 1967.

649 Economic Development in the Backward Countries. (A Dissenter's Guide to Foreign Policy. Ed. by Irving Howe. New York & Washington 1968, pp. 195—207.) [Cf. 563.]

650 An Economist's Vision of a Sane World. (Man and His World. The Noranda Lectures. Expo 67 ... Toronto 1968, pp. 17—27.) [Cf. 564, 912.]

651 An Essay in International Cooperation. (Now 5: 4—6. 1968, pp. 5—7.)

652 Five Generations of American Youth. (Now 5: 8. 1968, pp. 8—11.)

653 Gandhi as a Radical Liberal. (Mahatma Gandhi 100 Years. Ed. S. Radhakrishnan ... New Delhi 1968, pp. 260—269.) [Identical with 704, 920. Cf. 921.]

654 International Inequalities. (Expansion of World Trade and the Growth of National Economies: Significant Papers. Ed. by Richard S. Weckstein. New York 1968, pp. 61—77.) [Cf. 255a.]
Repr. of Economic Theory and Under-Developed Regions. Chapter 5. (257, 417)

656 Isolamento político e moral dos Estados Unidos. (532: 34)

657 Jag tror på framtiden. [I Believe in the Future.] (Nytt i Nacka 1968: 2, p. 7.)

658 Johnson och jordskredet. [President Lyndon B. Johnson and the Landslide.] (VeckoJournalen 1968: 14, pp. 16—17, 40.)

659 A Methodological Note on Valuations and Beliefs. (A Preface to Our Times. Contemporary Thought in Traditional Rhetorical Forms. [Ed. by] William E. Buckler. New York 1968, pp. 527—536.) [Cf. 141.]
An American Dilemma: Appendix 1. [Cf. 127a.]

660 Den "mjuka staten" i underutvecklade länder. [Orig. title: The "Soft State" in Under-Developed Countries.] (Nordisk Administrativt Tidsskrift 49 (1968), pp. 259—274.) [Cf. 668, 709.]
Adaptation from a lecture given in the Swedish section of the Nordiska Administrativa Förbundet on April 24th, 1968.

661 The Necessity and Difficulty of Planning the Future Society. (Environment and Change . . . Ed. by William R. Ewald, Jr. Bloomington & London 1968, pp. 250—263.) [Cf. 941.] [Not entirely identical with 662.]
Address, October 3, 1967, Washington, D. C., to the National Consultation on the Future Environment of a Democracy of the American Institute of Planners.

662 Necessity and Difficulty of Planning the Future Society. (Economic Planning Vol. 4: No. 3—4. May—July 1968, pp. 3—4, 6—9.) [Not entirely identical with 661.]

663 Objektivitetsproblemet i samhällsforskningen. [Orig. title:] Objectivity in Social Research. Övers. av [Transl. from the author's ms. by] Bo Lindensjö & Helena Siling. Stockholm, Rabén & Sjögren, & Helsingfors, Söderström, 1968, 95 pp. (Rabén & Sjögrens samhällsvetenskapliga bibliotek.) [Cf. 712c—713.]

664 Perspektiven der amerikanischen Rassenkrise. [Orig. title: The Racial Crisis in Perspective.] (Sozialistische Hefte 7 (1968), pp. 393—398.) [Cf. 587.]

665 Political Factors Affecting East-West Trade in Europe. (Co-Existence 5 (1968), pp. 141—148.) [Identical with 716, 948. Cf. 622.]

666 **Rich Lands, Poor Lands, and the Widening Gap. (From Underdevelopment to Affluence. Western, Soviet, and Chinese Views. Ed. by Harry G. Shaffer and Jan S. Prybyla. New York 1968, pp. 45—48.)**

667 The Social Sciences and Their Impact on Society. [With] Commentary. By Julia J. Henderson, Eveline M. Burns [&] George F. Rohrlich. [With] Response by Gunnar Myrdal. (Social Theory and Social Invention. Ed. . . . by Herman D. Stein. Cleveland 1968, pp. 143—179, 184—187.) [Cf. 867, 956.]

Lecture at the Fifteenth Anniversary Celebration of the School of Applied Social Sciences, Western Reserve University, Cleveland, Ohio, September 29—October 1, 1966.

668 The "Soft State" in Underdeveloped Countries. (UCLA Law Review 15 (1968), pp. 1118—1134.)

Lecture 17 February, 1968, at a Conference arranged by the Faculty of Law at the University of California, Los Angeles . . . — Adaptation of a paper contributed to a volume in honor of Thomas Balogh. . . (767)

669 The Soft States. (The Asia Magazine 8 (1968): 24, pp. 3—9.)
Excerpts from Asian Drama. (637)

670 Sosiaaliset arvot ja niiden universaalisuus. [Orig. title: Social Values and Their Universality.] (Kasvatus ja koulu 54 (1968), pp. 191—200.) [Cf. 722.]

671 [Tal vid ett möte som anordnades av Svenska kommittén för Vietnam den 21 februari 1968 på Sergels torg i Stockholm.] [Speech at a meeting arranged by the Swedish Committee for Vietnam . . .] (Röster för Vietnam. Stockholm, Svenska kommittén för Vietnam, 1968, p. 3.)

672 Too Late to Plan? (Bulletin of the Atomic Scientists, January 1968, pp. 5—9.) [Cf. 661.]

The article is based upon an address presented to the American Institute of Planners, October 3, 1967.

673+ Twenty Years of the United Nations Economic Commission for Europe. (International Organization 22 (1968), pp. 617—628.) [Cf. 962.]

Rev. version of an address delivered on April 12, 1967, in the Palais des Nations, Geneva, commemorating the Twentieth Anniversary of the Commission. [Cf. 553.]

674 * Utväg ur Vietnam? [How to Get Out of Vietnam?] [With] Kenneth Galbraith [&] Robert F. Kennedy. Gunnar Myrdals avsnitt översatta av [G. M.'s chapters transl. by] Olof Hoffsten. Stockholm, Rabén & Sjögren, Tema, 1968, 120 pp. (458: Den dåraktiga utrikespolitiken. — 676: Vietnamkriget och Förenta staternas politiska och moraliska isolering. — 675: Vietnam — ett moraliskt problem för hela världen.)

675 Vietnam — ett moraliskt problem för hela världen. (606: 11)

676 Vietnamkriget och Förenta staternas politiska och moraliska isolering. (532: 35)

677 Western Economic Warfare 1947—1967. (Now 5: 13. 1968, pp. 8—9.) [Cf. 678.]

678¹ [Foreword to:] Adler-Karlsson, Gunnar: Western Economic Warfare 1947—1967 ... Stockholm 1968, pp. XI—XIII. [Cf. 770—771.]

678² [Introduction to:] McCarthy, Eugene J.: Vad är viktigast? Behov och resurser i USA. Ett program för att i en svår tid ena nationen. [Orig. title: First Things First.] Stockholm 1968, pp. 7—8.

679 As opções políticas do desenvolvimento econômico. [The Political Options of the Economic Development.] (Folha de S. Paulo 13/10 1968. Caderno especial.)

680 Skillnaden mellan rika och fattiga bara ökar — det är det tragiska asiatiska dramat. [The Distance between the Rich and the Poor Only Increases — That Is the Tragic Asian Drama.] (Expressen 11/3 1968.)
Excerpt from the Swedish transl. of Asian Drama (643), Chap. 16, "Equality and Democracy."

681 Stärk opinionen mot Vietnamkriget — men gör det med värdiga demokratiska metoder! [Fortify the Opinion against the War in Vietnam — But Do It with Dignified Democratic Methods!] (Arbetaren 47 (1968): 5, pp. 3, 10; 9, p. 4. [With discussion.]) [Cf. 682.]

682 Den svenska protesten mot USA:s Vietnampolitik. [The Swedish Protest against the Vietnam Policy of the US.] (Dagens Nyheter 25/1 1968.) [Cf. 681.]
Main address at the Inaugural Annual Meeting of the Swedish Committee for Vietnam, January 24, 1968. — With a reply in the Dagens Nyheter 9/2 1968 by James O. Batcha [pseud.].

683 There's a Rising Trend to Violence. (Winnipeg Free Press, June 8, 1968.)

684 USA, Vietnamopinionen och den svenska regeringen. Svar på tal. [U. S. A., the Opinion on Vietnam and the Swedish Government. A Rejoinder. (Dagens Nyheter 29/2 1968.)
Reply to Elisabet Hermodsson's article USA, Vietnamopinionen och den svenska regeringen. Myrdals mardröm, in the Dagens Nyheter 29/2 1968.

685 Angeläget: Gunnar Myrdal. [Urgent . . .] (Böckernas värld 3 (1968): 3, pp. 4—5.)
Interview by Gustaf-Adolf Mannberg on account of the issue of Asian Drama. (637)

686 As I See It. (Forbes 101: 7. 1968, pp. 68—69.)
A Forbes Interview.

687[1] Canada Can Be Independent and Grow. (The Financial Post, Oct. 19, 1968.)
Interview by Paul Gibson.

687[2] Gunnar Myrdal on Poor People's March. (The Globe (Boston), May 26, 1968.)
Interview by Mike McGrady. [Cf. 781[1].]

688 Hur ska man hjälpa de fattiga länderna? VA frågar Gunnar Myrdal. [How to Aid the Underdeveloped Countries? . . .] (Veckans Affärer 14/3 1968, pp. 22—24, 34.)
Interview on account of the publication of Asian Drama. (637)

689 In Stockholm, Gunnar Myrdal Talks About the American Conscience with J. Robert Moskin. (Look 1968: December 24, pp. 32, 34—36.)
Interview.

690 An Interview with Gunnar Myrdal. (Phi Delta Kappan 49 (1968), pp. 490—494.)
Interview by Stanley Elam.

90

691 Mellan fyra ögon. [In Private.] (VeckoJournalen 1968: 13, pp. 26—29, 40.)
Interview by Lars Bringert.

692 Myrdal Finds Students Interested in World Affairs. (The Ohio State University Monthly 59: 5. January 1968, p. 8.)
Interview.

693 "The Only Thing We Can Do Is Try to Put Facts on the Table ..." (The Washington Post Book World, June 9, 1968, pp. 6—7.)
Interview in Stockholm by Milton Viorst.

694 Ska vi äta gräddtårta — eller hjälpa u-länder? [Sugar Trifle or Aid to the Under-Developed Countries?] (Kamratposten 77 (1968): 10, pp. 10—11.)
Short interview with Katarina Hennicks and Lisbeth Karlsson.

695 Världen är sjuk! [The world is sick!] (Röster i radio-TV 1968: 20, pp. 14—15, 51.)
Interview by Matts Rying.

696 What Has Roused Youth? (Lithopinion 3: 3. Issue 11. 1968, pp. 2—11.)
Interview in New York City by Samuel Grafton.

1969

697 An American Dilemma. The Negro Problem and Modern Democracy. With the assistance of Richard Sterner and Arnold Rose. Vol. 1—2. New York, Evanston & London, Harper & Row, 1969, pp. I—LXXXIII, 1—520, 1181—1335, 1441—1484; pp. I—XII, 523—1180, 1335 (!)—1483. (Harper Torchbooks 1443—44.) [Cf. 127d, 808, 1015.]
As to pagination irregularities see Vol. 1, p. [IV], note.

698 Asiatisk drama. En undersøkelse av nasjonenes fattigdom. Politiske problemer i Syd-Asia. [Orig. title:] Asian Drama. An Inquiry into the Poverty of Nations. Political Problems in South Asia. Overs. av [Transl. from the Swedish condensed ed. by] Truls Hoff. Oslo, Gyldendal, 1969, 387 pp. (Gyldendals kjempefakler K 21.) [Cf. 641 f.]
This ed. corresponds to P. 2 and P. 4: Chapter 16 of Asian Drama. (637)

699   Asiatiskt drama. En undersökning om nationernas fattig-
      dom. [Orig. title:] Asian Drama. An Inquiry into the
      Poverty of Nations. Stockholm, Rabén & Sjögren, [Helsing-
      fors, Söderström]. (Skrifter utg. av Utrikespolitiska institutet.)
      [Cf. 637.]
      [1.] Politiska problem i Sydasien. [Political Problems in South Asia.]
      Bemyndigad övers. av [Authorized transl. by] Roland Adlerberth.
      3rd ed. 1969, VIII, 367 pp. [Cf. 643, 736.]

700   Challenge to Affluence. The Emergence of an "Under-Class"
      (Structured Social Inequality. A Reader in Comparative
      Social Stratification. Ed. and with an introd. by Celia S.
      Heller. New York . . . 1969, pp. 138—143.) [Identical with
      460.]

701   Cleansing the Approach from Biases in the Study of Under-
      developed Countries. (Social Science Information 8 (1969):
      3, pp. 9—26.) [Cf. 741.]
      "This paper is a draft to the introductory chapter of the book which will
      be published by Pantheon Books, New York, The Challenge of World
      Poverty". (739a)

702   Ekonomisk teori och underutvecklade regioner. [Orig. title:]
      Economic Theory and Underdeveloped Regions. Övers.
      [Transl.]: James Rössel. Stockholm, Tiden, 1969, 180 pp.
      [Cf. 255e.]
      New ed. (with a new Preface) of Rika och fattiga länder. (266)

703   L'état "mou" dans les pays sous-développés. [Orig. title:
      The "Soft State" in Underdeveloped Countries.] (Revue
      Tiers-Monde 10: 37. 1969, pp. 5—24.) [Cf. 668.]

704   Gandhi as a Radical Liberal. (Now 5: 22. 1969, pp. 6—9.)
      [Identical with 653, 920.]

705   The Intergovernmental Organizations and the Role of their
      Secretariats. (Canadian Public Administration. Journal . . .
      12 (1969): 313—333.) [Cf. 714, 933.]
      The Institute of Public Administration of Canada, Toronto. — The
      W. Clifford Clark Memorial Lecture, 1969.

706   An International Economy. Problems and Prospects. [New
      ed.] New Preface by the author. New York, Harper & Row,
      1969, 381 pp. (Harper Torchbooks 1445.) [Cf. 244c.]

707 "Investment in Man." (International Social Work 12:4. 1969, pp. 2—15.)
Reimpression of chapter 29 in the author's Asian Drama. (637)

708 Låt vietnameserna själva råda över sitt land! [Let the Vietnamese Govern Their Country Themselves!] (Vietnam 69 ... Red. av Bertil Svahnström. Stockholm 1969, pp. 11—14.)

709 Den mjuka staten i underutvecklade länder. [Orig. title: The "Soft State" in Under-Developed Countries.] [Transl. from the author's manuscript by Kerstin Lundgren.] (U-hjälp i utveckling? 14 forskare och samhällsvetare om Sveriges u-landspolitik och utvecklingsbistånd. Utg. i samarbete med SIDA ... Stockholm & Helsingfors 1969, pp. 15—29.) (W&W serien 209.) [Cf. 767.]

710 The Negro School: A Swedish Analysis. (American Education in Foreign Perspectives. Twentieth Century Essays. Comp. and ed. by Stewart E. Fraser. New York ... 1969, pp. 95—117.)
Repr. from An American Dilemma ... New York 1944, pp. 879—886, 893—987. [Cf. 127a.]

711+ Objectivity in Social Research. Latrobe, Pa., The Archabbey Press, [1969], VIII, 111 pp. (Wimmer Lecture 21.) [Cf. 712.]
Expanded version of the Wimmer Lecture, delivered at St. Vincent College, Latrobe, Pa., 1967.

712a —New York, Pantheon Books, [1969], VIII, 111 pp. (The 1967 Wimmer Lecture, St. Vincent College, Latrobe, Pa.) [Cf. 711.]

712b — London [1970]. (755)

712c Translations.
[Dutch. Cf. 1051.]
[German:] Objektivität in der Sozialforschung. Frankfurt am Main 1971. (810)
[Italian:] L'obiettività nelle scienze sociali. Torino 1973. (944)

[Japanese:] Shakai kagaku to kachi handan. Tōkyō 1971. (820)
[Portuguese. Cf. 1051.]
[Spanish:] Objetividad en la investigación social. México 1970. (756)
[Swedish:] Objektivitetsproblemet i samhällsforskningen. Stockholm 1968. (663)
[—] — 2:a uppl. Stockholm 1969. (713)

713　Objektivitetsproblemet i samhällsforskningen. [Orig. title:] Objectivity in Social Research. Övers. av [Transl. [from the author's ms.] by] Bo Lindensjö & Helena Siling. 2:a uppl. [2nd ed.] Stockholm, Rabén & Sjögren, 1969, 95 pp. (Rabén & Sjögrens samhällsvetenskapliga bibliotek.) [Cf. 663, 712c.] 2nd pr. 1970.

714　Les organisations intergouvernementales et le rôle de leurs secrétariats. (Administration publique du Canada. Journal of the Institute of Public Administration of Canada. 12 (1969), pp. 334—355.) [Cf. 705.]
Les Conférences commémoratives W. Clifford Clark 1969.

715　The Political Element in the Development of Economic Theory. Transl. from German [Das politische Element in der nationalökonomischen Doktrinbildung] by Paul Streeten. New York, Simon and Shuster, 1969, XVIII, 249 pp. (A Clarion Book.) [Cf. 11c, 26.]

716　Political Factors Affecting East-West Trade in Europe. (Now 5: 18. 1969, pp. 5—9.) [Identical with 665, 948.]

717　Population. A Problem for Democracy. Magnolia, Mass., Smith, 1969, 238 pp. [Cf. 94b.]
Facs. ed.

718　Public Workers: A Developing Resource in the Underdeveloped Nations. (ADA World 4 (1969): 3, pp. 1—2.) [Cf. 721.]

719　De rika ländernas ansvar och möjlighet att hjälpa de underutvecklade länderna i deras utvecklingspolitik. [The Responsibility and Means of the Rich Countries to Aid the

Poor Countries in Their Policy of Development.] (Bedrifts-økonomen 31 (1969): 4, pp. 157—159, 161.)
Shortened version of a lecture at the Norwegian University of Commerce, Bergen, 1968.

720 The Role and Reality of Race. (Now 5: 31. 1969, pp. 10—11.) [Cf. 818, 953.]
Luncheon speech at the Convocation "Toward the Year 2018", called by the Foreign Policy Association ..., New York, May 28, 1968.

721 The Role of the Public Services in Underdeveloped Countries. (Economic Planning 5 (1969): 5, pp. 3—6. — Public Services International Bulletin, February 1969, pp. 1—9.) [Cf. 718, 757, 955.]
Lecture at the Second Asian Regional Conference of Public Services International in Singapore, November 14, 1968.

722 Social Values and Their Universality. (International Social Work 12: 1. 1969, pp. 3—11.) [Cf. 670.]
Opening Address at the 14th International Congress of Schools of Social Work, Helsinki, Finland, August 14th, 1968.

723 Der „Soft State" in den Entwicklungsländern. [Orig. title: The "Soft State" in Underdeveloped Countries.] (Viertel-jahresberichte Nr. 36. Juni 1969, pp. 121—136. [With English and French summaries.]) [Cf. 767.]

724 The "Soft State" in Underdeveloped Countries. (Now, August 8. 1969, pp. 6—8.) [Cf. 668.]

725 The Soft States of South Asia: The Civil Servant Problem. (Bulletin of the Atomic Scientists, April 1969, pp. 7—10.) [Cf. 721.]

726 To Young Americans with Love. (Americans for Democratic Action. 22nd Annual Convention 1969, 6 pp.)
Address to Temple University's 1968 graduating class.

728 Världsekonomin. Övers. från förf:s engelska manuskript av Leif Björk. [Med nytt förord av förf.] [An International Economy. Transl. ... With new Preface by the author.] [New ed.] Stockholm, Tiden, 1969, 467 pp. [Cf. 244d, 247.]

729 Dong So Gyoyok Kwa Gu Zongchizok Yogu. [East-West Trade and Its Political Ingredients.] (The Dong-A Ilbo 11/1 1969.) [Cf. 622.]
Title and text in Korean.

730 Gunnar Myrdal realist eller idealist? (Folktidningen Ny Tid 23/1 1969.)
From an interview and debate in Nyland's Nation, University of Helsinki.

731 Witness to the Asian drama. 'A Tragedy to See Poor Countries Spending so Much Money on Arms.' (The Asia Magazine 9 (1969): 1, pp. 38—43.)
Interview.

1970

732 Address Delivered at the Inaugural Meeting of the One Asia Assembly, Manila, April 11, 1970. (914: Essays and Lectures, pp. 233—239.)

733 A Agricultura e a Revolução Econômica do Mundo. [Orig. title: The United Nations, Agriculture, and the World Economic Revolution.] (769: Subdesenvolvimento, pp. 33—43.) [Cf. 483.]

734+ Agricultural Development and Planning in Underdeveloped Countries Outside the Socialist Sphere. National Purpose, Methods, Difficulties and Results. (Economic Planning. Journal for Agriculture and Related Industries 6 (1970): 3/4, pp. 3—7.) [Cf. 782, 784, 799, 897.]
Paper prepared for the International Association of Agricultural Economists Conference in Minsk, USSR, 23 August—3 September, 1970.

735 An Approach to the Asian Drama. Methodological and Theoretical. Selections from Asian Drama. An Inquiry into the Poverty of Nations . . . Principal assistants: William J. Barber, Altti Majava, Alva Myrdal, Paul P. Streeten, David Wightman, George W. Wilson. New York, Vintage Books, 1970, XVI, 680 pp. (A Vintage Giant 573.) [Cf. 637, 641b.]

736 Asiatiskt drama. En undersökning om nationernas fattigdom. [Orig. title:] Asian Drama. An Inquiry into the Poverty of

Nations. Stockholm, Rabén & Sjögren, [Helsingfors, Söderström]. (Skrifter utg. av Utrikespolitiska Institutet.) [Cf. 637.]

2. Ekonomiska och sociala problem i Sydasien. [Economic and Social Problems in South Asia.] [Adaptation and abridgment of parts of the Asian Drama by] Kjell Eriksson, Horst Hart, Benny Hjern. 1970, 254 pp.
3. Arbetskraftens utnyttjande. [Labour Utilization.] [Adaptation and abridgment of parts of the Asian Drama by] Kjell Eriksson, Horst Hart, Benny Hjern. 1970, 317 pp. [Cf. 643, 699.]

737+ Biases in Social Research. (The Place of Value in a World of Facts. Proceedings of the Fourteenth Nobel Symposium, Stockholm, September 15—20, 1969. Ed. by Arne Tiselius & Sam Nilsson. Stockholm, New York, London & Sydney 1970, pp. 155—161.) [Cf. 914.]

738 The Challenge of Agriculture. (The Asia Magazine 10 (1970): 38, pp. 16—17, 26—27, 32—33.) [Cf. 734.]

739a+ The Challenge of World Poverty. A World Anti-Poverty Program in Outline. With a Foreword by Francis O. Wilcox. New York, Pantheon Books, 1970, XVIII, 518 pp. [Cf. 701, 761, 805—806.]

The Christian A. Herter Lecture Series. — A summary and continuation of Asian Drama. (637)

739b — London, Allen Lane The Penguin Press, 1970, 518 pp.

739c — Harmondsworth 1971. (791)

739d — New York 1971. (790)

739e Translations.
[Danish:] Om verdensfattigdommen. København 1972. (860)
[Dutch:] De misdeelde wereld. Antwerpen 1971. (803)
[French:] Le défi du monde pauvre. Paris 1971. (792)
[German:] Politisches Manifest über die Armut in der Welt. Frankfurt am Main 1970. (759a)
[—] — Gekürzte Ausg. Frankfurt am Main 1972. (864)
[Hindi:] Viśva nirdhantā kī cunautī. Dillī & Patnā 1976. (1055)
[Hungarian:] Korunk kihívása: a világszegénység. Budapest 1974. (993)

97

[Italian:] La sfida del mondo povero. Milano 1976. (1054)
[Japanese:] Hinkon kara no chōsen. Tōkyō 1971. (798)
[Korean:] Pin'gon-ŭi tojŏn. Seoul 1977. (1071)
[Spanish:] Reto a la pobreza. Barcelona 1973. (952)
[Swedish:] Politiskt manifest om världsfattigdomen. Stock-holm 1970. (760)
[Urdu. Cf. 1047.]

740 A Classe Submersa na Grande Sociedade. [Orig. title: The Under Class in the Great Society.] (769: Subdesenvolvimento, pp. 45—58.) [Cf. 481.]

741 Cleansing the Approach from Biases in the Study of Under-developed Countries. (Studium Generale 23 (1970), pp. 1249—66.) [Cf. 701.]

742 [Contribution to the debate on the paper] Treatment of the Nutrition Problems in the Science of Economics. By J. Vogt. (Evaluation of Novel Protein Products ... Ed. by A. E. Bender ... Oxford ... 1970, pp. 12—13.) (Wenner-Gren Center International Symposium Series 14.)
Proceedings of the International Biological Programme (IBP) and Wen-ner-Gren Center Symposium held in Stockholm, September 1968. Session 1.

743 [Contribution to the] Panel Discussion: Science and the World Food Problem. (Evaluation of Novel Protein Products ... Ed. by A. E. Bender ... Oxford ... 1970, pp. 367—377.) (Wenner-Gren Center International Symposium Series 14.)
Proceedings of the International Biological Programme (IBP) and Wen-ner-Gren Center Symposium held in Stockholm, September 1968. Session 1.

744 The Effects of Social Inequality. (Being Black: Psychological-Sociological Dilemmas. [Ed. by] Robert V. Guthrie. San Francisco 1970, pp. 130—145.)
From An American Dilemma, pp. 640—644. (127a)

745[1] Esforços no Sentido da Integração de Paises Ricos e Pobres. [Orig. title: The Effects Toward Integration in Rich and

Poor Countries.] (769: Subdesenvolvimento, pp. 81—95.) [Cf. 503.]

745² Etiken i utvecklingsarbetet. [Ethics in Developmental Work.] (Världen och värdena. Föredrag och rapporter vid 29:e allmänna kyrkliga mötet i Jönköping 1970 . . . Stockholm 1970, pp. 126—129.)

746 Forskningens och det teknologiska utvecklingsarbetets roll i utvecklingen av underutvecklade länder. [The Role of Research-Work and Technological Work of Development in the Progress of Underdeveloped Countries.] (Forskning och framtid. TCO:s utbildningsdagar 1970. [Stockholm 1970], pp. 38—47.)

747 Free Trade and Inequality. From Rich Lands and Poor, 1957 . . . (Perspectives on the Economic Problem. A Book of Readings in Political Economy. Ed. by Arthur MacEwan and Thomas E. Weisskopf. Englewood Cliffs, N.J., 1970, pp. 260—264.) [Cf. 265a.]

748 Fukushi kokka wo koete. Fukushi kokka deno keizai keikaku to sono kokusaiteki imi kanren. [Japanese transl. of: Beyond the Welfare State. Economic Planning in the Welfare States . . .] Chief of compilation: Kazuo Kitagawa. Joint transl.: Itsuo Kawamura and Yoshio Matsunaga. Tōkyō, Diamond Inc., 1970, 371 pp. [Cf. 323e, 392.]

749¹ Gunā Myurudāru hakushi kōen-shū. NHK hen. [Collected Lectures by Gunnar Myrdal. Publ. by NHK.] Tōkyō 1970, 58 pp.
Contents: Kōfuku no keizai-tetsugaku. (749²—750) — Nanaju-nendai no Ajia no dorama. (754) — Keizai-daikoku Nihon e ichigon. (780)

749² Kōfuku no keizai tetsugaku. Jinrui no shinpo to chōwa no sekai wo motomete. [Orig. title: Is the World on the Road to Progress and Harmony for Mankind?] (Gunā Myurudāru hakushi kōen-shū. [Collected Lectures by Gunnar Myrdal.] Tōkyō 1970, pp. 7—26.) [Identical with 750. Cf. 754, 780.]
Lecture prepared for NHK on April 6th, 1970, in connection with the World Exposition in Osaka, Japan.

750 Kōfuku no keizai tetsugaku. Jinrui no shinpo to chōwa no sekai wo motomete. [Followed by the English original text:] Is the World on the Road to Progress and Harmony for Mankind? (Mirai no tame no shisaku. — Contemplations for Better Tomorrow. Lectures . . . [Osaka] 1970, pp. 349—360; 361—370.) [Identical with 749². Cf. 754, 780.]

751 A Mad World. (Impact 5 (1970): 6, pp. 4—9.)
P. 1: Transcript of a lecture given at the University of the Philippines, April 13, 1970.

752 Mass Poverty & Green Revolution. (Business Man 12: 1 (November 1970), pp. 33—40, 32.) [Identical with 814.]
Introductory Address at the Plenary Session of the Third International Congress of Food Science and Technology, August 10th, 1970, in Washington, D. C.

753 A Modern View of the Problem. (Economic Development and Population Growth. A Conflict? Ed. with introd. by H. Peter Gray & Shanti S. Tangri. Lexington, Mass., 1970, pp. 23—28.)
A passage from the 1965 McDougall Memorial Lecture to the Food and Agricultural Organization of the United Nations on Nov. 22, 1965. [Cf. 495.]

754 Nanaju-nendai no Ajia no dorama. Namboku mondai no mirai zo. [Asian Drama in the 1970's. The Future of the North-South Question.] (Gunā Myurudāru hakushi kōen-shū. [Collected Lectures by Gunnar Myrdal.] Tōkyō 1970, pp. 27—45.) [Cf. 749¹—750, 780.]
Lecture prepared for NHK on April 6th, 1970, in connection with the World Exposition in Osaka, Japan.

755 Objectivity in Social Research. London, Duckworth, [1970], VIII, 111 pp. [Cf. 711.]

756 Objetividad en la investigación social. [Orig. title:] Objectivity in Social Research. Trad. de Remigio Jasso. México, Fondo de cultura económica, 1970, 119 pp. (Breviarios del Fondo de cultura económica 212.) [Cf. 712c.]

757 O Papel dos Serviços Públicos nos Paises Subdesenvolvidos. [Orig. title: The Role of the Public Services in Under-

developed Countries.] (769: Subdesenvolvimento, pp. 125—139.) [Cf. 721.]

758   The Policeman in the Negro Neighborhood. (The Black Man and the Promise of America. Ed. by Lettie J. Austin, Lewis H. Fenderson, Sophia P. Nelson. Glenview, Ill., 1970, pp. 159—160.)
From An American Dilemma, pp. 540—542. (127a)

759a   Politisches Manifest über die Armut in der Welt. [Orig. title:] The Challenge of World Poverty. Aus dem Amerikanischen von Suzanne Reichstein. Frankfurt am Main, Suhrkamp, 1970, XV, 496 pp. [Cf. 739e, 800.]

759b   — Gekürzte Ausg. . . . Frankfurt am Main 1972. (864)

760   Politiskt manifest om världsfattigdomen. En sammanfattning och fortsättning av Asiatiskt drama. [Orig. title: The Challenge of World Poverty. A Summary and Continuation of Asian Drama.] Övers. av [Transl. by] Kerstin Lundgren. Stockholm, Rabén & Sjögren, 1970, 364 pp. [Cf. 739e.]

761   Population and Resources from "The Challenge of World Poverty". (Ceres 3: 1. 1970, pp. 51—61.)
Corresponds to pp. 139—163 of The Challenge of World Poverty, 1970. [Cf. 739a.]

762   Prioridade nos Esforços de Desenvolvimento. [Orig. title: Priorities in the Development Efforts of Underdeveloped Countries and Their Trade and Financial Relations with Rich Countries.] (769: Subdesenvolvimento, pp. 13—31.) [Cf. 427.]

763   Recreation. (Recreation and Leisure Service for the Disadvantaged. Guidelines to Program Development and Related Things. Ed. by John A. Nesbitt . . . Philadelphia 1970, p. 35 ff.)
Corresponds to pp. 982—986 in An American Dilemma. (410)

764   [Rede anlässlich der Verleihung des Friedenspreises des Börsenvereins des Deutschen Buchhandels, Frankfurt am Main, in der Paulskirche am 27.9. 1970.] (Börsenblatt für

den Deutschen Buchhandel 26 (1970), pp. 2305—2310. — Alva und Gunnar Myrdal. Ansprachen ... Frankfurt am Main 1970, pp. 39—56.) [Cf. 825.]

765 Reforma Agrária em seu Sentido Amplo, Social e Econômico. [Orig. title: Land Reform in Its Broader Economic and Social Setting.] (769: Subdesenvolvimento, pp. 59—79.) [Cf. 509.]

766 Reply [to Some Comments on the Treatment of the Problems of the Inadequate Statistics of South Asia Countries in Asian Drama by Gunnar Myrdal. By J. Edward Ely]. (The Journal of Economic Literature 8 (1970), pp. 52—53.

767+ The 'Soft State' in Underdeveloped Countries. (Unfashionable Economics. Essays in honour of Lord Balogh. Ed. by Paul Streeten. London 1970, pp. 227—243.) [Cf. 660, 668, 703, 709, 723—724, 768.]

768 O Soft State. [Orig. title: The 'Soft State' in Underdeveloped Countries.] (769: Subdesenvolvimento, pp. 97—123.) [Cf. 668.]

769 Subdesenvolvimento. Trad. e adapt. Rosinethe Monteiro Soares. Rev. Nicoletta Viale Tavares e José M. Mattos Velloso. Brasília, Coordenada Editôra de Brasília, 1970, 139 pp. (Coleção Gunnar Myrdal 1.)
Contents: Prioridade nos Esforços de Desenvolvimento. (762) — A Agricultura e a Revolução Econômica do Mundo. (733) — A Classe Submersa na Grande Sociedade. (740) — Reforma Agrária em seu Sentido Amplo, Social e Econômico. (765) — Esforços no Sentido da Integração de Paises Ricos e Pobres. (745¹) — O Soft State. (768) — O Papel dos Serviços Públicos nos Paises Subdesenvolvidos. (757)

---

770 [Foreword to:] Adler-Karlsson, Gunnar: Västerns ekonomiska krigföring 1947—1967. [Western Economic Warfare 1947—1967.] Stockholm 1970, pp. 7—12. [Cf. 678¹.]

771 [Foreword to:] Adler-Karlsson, Gunnar: Vestblokkens økonomiske krigføring 1947—1967 ... [Western Economic Warfare 1947—1967.] Overs. av [Transl. by] Kristian Gleditsch. Oslo 1970, pp. 9—13. [Extract.] [Cf. 678¹.]

772 [Foreword to:] Matzner, Egon: Trade between East and West. Stockholm 1970. p. [5]. (Stockholm Economic Studies. New Series XII.)

773 [Foreword to:] Wirt, Frederick M.: Politics of Southern Equality. Law and Social Change in a Mississippi County. Chicago 1970, pp. VII—VIII.

774 Omöjligt att "blixt-industrialisera" underutvecklat land. Arbetslösheten är största problemet. [Impossible to "Blitz-Industrialize" Underdeveloped Countries. Unemployment Is the Biggest Problem.] (Arbetet 26/10 1970.) [Continuation of 775. Continued by 776.]

775 Teknisk hjälp till underutvecklade länder räcker inte. Satsa på social utvecklingshjälp. [Technical Help to Underdeveloped Countries Is Not Enough. Stake on Social Help to Further the Development.] (Arbetet 25/10 1970.) [Continued by 774.]

776 Vad kan vi göra för de underutvecklade länderna? Dela med oss av våra kunskaper. [What Can We Do for the Underdeveloped Countries? Let Them Share Our Knowledge.] (Arbetet 27/10 1970.) [Continuation of 774.]

777 Gunnar Myrdal. En intervju av Nordal Åkerman. [An Interview by . . .] (Internationell makt och förtryck. Red.: Nordal Åkerman. Stockholm & Helsingfors 1970, pp. 33—41.) [Identical with 633.]

778 Gunnar Myrdal: International Prophet. [Report of an interview.] (Nonaligned Third World Annual 1970, pp. 19—22.) Interviewers: Susan Stone and Iqbal A. Siddiqi. The interview took place in Stockholm on May 20, 1970. — The report is followed by a short bibliography of Myrdal's works (pp. 23—29).

779 Interview mit Professor Gunnar Myrdal. Aus dem Englischen übersetzte Auszüge der Tonbandaufzeichnung eines Gesprächs vom 24. Juli 1969. (Darmstädter Blätter 2. 1970, pp. 33—39.)

780 Keizai-daikoku Nihon e ichigon. [A Word about Japan as Economic World Power.] (Gunā Myurudāru hakushi kōen-shū. [Collected Lectures by Gunnar Myrdal.] Tōkyō 1970, pp. 47—57.) [Cf. 749[1], 750, 754.]
Interview prepared for NHK on April 6th, 1970. — Interviewer: Kiyoshi Tsuchiya.

781[1] Poverty and Political Action. (Poverty in Affluence. Ed. by Robert E. Will & Harold G. Vatter. 2nd ed. New York 1970, pp. 209—210.)
From an interview in the Globe (Boston) by Mike McGrady. (687[2])

781[2] Sverige förlorar på sin ärlighet. [Sweden Loses because of Being Honest.] (Dagens Nyheter 28/9 1970.)
Interview by Svante Nycander.

1971

782 Agricultural Development and Planning in the Under-developed Countries Outside the Socialist Sphere. National Purpose, Methods, Difficulties and Results. (Institute for International Economic Studies, University of Stockholm. Reprint Series 1. [1971, 9 pp.]) [Cf. 734.]

783 America at the Crossroads. (Law and Change in Modern America. Ed. by Joel B. Grossman and Mary H. Grossman. Pacific Palisades, Calif., 1971, pp. 223—240.)
Corresponds to pp. 997—1004, 1010—15, 1018—24 in An American Dilemma. (127a)

784 Are the Developing Countries Really Developing? (Bulletin of the Atomic Scientists 27 (1971): 1, pp. 5—8.)
The paper upon which this article is based was presented before the International Association of Agricultural Economists Conference in Minsk, USSR, 23 August—3 September, 1970. [Cf. 734.]

785 [Asian Drama.] (Ekonomiska Samfundets Tidskrift — The Journal of the Economic Society of Finland Ser. 3. 24 (1971), p. 145.)
Article written to the Editor of the Journal because of Jeja-Pekka Roos's review of Asian Drama.

786 Asian Drama. An Inquiry Into the Poverty of Nations. An Abridgment by Seth S. King of The Twentieth Century Fund Study. [Foreword by M. J. Rossant.] New York, Pantheon Books, 1971, XIII, 464 pp. [Cf. 641c, 847—848.]

787 [Asian Drama.] Replikväxling Gunnar Myrdal — Johan Åkerman. [Exchange of Views . . .] (Statsvetenskaplig Tidskrift 74 (1971), pp. 87—89.)
Some remarks about the authorship of Asian Drama. (637)

788 Entry cancelled.

789 Aufsätze und Reden. [Auswahl] aus dem Englischen übers. von Michael Lang. Frankfurt am Main, Suhrkamp, 1971, 155 pp. (Ed. Suhrkamp 492.)
Contents: Die Landwirtschaft und die Revolution der Weltwirtschaft. (802) — Die Landreform in ihrem grösseren wirtschaftlichen und sozialen Rahmen. (801) — Stimmt etwas nicht mit dem Wohlfahrtsstaat? (821) — Der Vietnamkrieg und die politische und moralische Isolierung Amerikas. (532: 36) — Vietnam — ein moralisches Problem für die Welt. (606: 12) — Rolle und Realität der Rasse. (818) — Noch einmal: Ein amerikanisches Dilemma. Die Rassenkrise in den Vereinigten Staaten in historischer Perspektive. (809)

790 The Challenge of World Poverty. A World Anti-Poverty Program in Outline. New York, Vintage, 1971, XVIII, 531 pp. (Vintage Books 170.) [Cf. 739d.]

791 — A World Anti-Poverty Programme in Outline. Foreword by Francis O. Wilcox. Harmondsworth, Penguin Books, 1971, 464 pp. (Pelican Books.) [Cf. 739c.]

792 Le défi du monde pauvre. Un programme de lutte sur le plan mondial. Titre original: The Challenge of World Poverty. A World Anti-Poverty Program in Outline. Trad. par Guy Durand. Paris, Gallimard, 1971, 465 pp. (Bibliothèque des sciences humaines.) [Cf. 739e.]

793[1] The Economic Impact of Colonialism. (Developing the Underdeveloped Countries. Ed. by Alan B. Mountjoy. London . . . 1971, pp. 52—57.) [Cf. 1020.]

793² Economic Inequality. (Black Americans and White Business. Ed. by Edwin M. Epstein & David R. Hampton. Encino, Calif., 1971, pp. 18—27.)
From An American Dilemma, pp. 205—219. (127a)

794 Economic Theory and Underdeveloped Regions. New York . . ., London, Harper & Row, 1971, XII, 168 pp. (Harper Torchbooks 1564.) [Cf. 255d.]

795 Entwickeln sich die unterentwickelten Länder tatsächlich? (Neue Wege 65 (1971), pp. 79—83.) [Cf. 734.]

796 Etelä-Aasia. Köyhien maanosa. Gunnar Myrdalin Asian Drama-teoksen pohjalta toimittanut ja suomentanut Lyyli Virtanen. [South Asia. The Continent of the Poor. Ed. and transl. by . . .] Helsinki, Weilin & Göös, 1971, 83 pp.
Adaptation of Asian Drama. (637)

797 Facets of the Negro Problem. (Racism. A Casebook. Ed. by Frederick R. Lapides [&] David J. Burrows. New York 1971, pp. 74—86.) [Cf. 280.]
Corresponds to pp. 50—60 in An American Dilemma. (127a)

798 Hinkon kara no chōsen. [Japanese transl. of: The Challenge of World Poverty. A World Anti-Poverty Program in Outline.] Chief of compilation: Saburo Okita. 1—2. Tōkyō, Diamond Inc., 1971, 282+230 pp. [Cf. 739e.]

799 Jordbruksutveckling och jordbruksplanering i de underutvecklade länderna utanför det socialistiska blocket. [Orig. title: Agricultural Development and Planning in the Underdeveloped Countries Outside the Socialist Sphere.] (Tiden 63 (1971), pp. 268—275, 291.) [Cf. 734.]

800 Kein Alibi, sondern eine Herausforderung. [From: The Challenge of World Poverty . . . German: Politisches Manifest über die Armut in der Welt. Frankfurt am Main 1970.] (Das Nord-Süd-Problem. Konflikte zwischen Industrie- und Entwicklungsländern. Hrsg. [von] Michael Bohnet. = Piper Sozialwissenschaft Bd 8. Red. Hans-Helmut Röhring. München 1971, pp. 102—109.) [Cf. 759a.]

801 Die Landreform in ihrem grösseren wirtschaftlichen und sozialen Rahmen. [Orig. title: Land Reform in Its Broader Economic and Social Setting.] (789: Aufsätze und Reden, pp. 22—39.) [Cf. 509.]

802 Die Landwirtschaft und die Revolution der Weltwirtschaft. [Orig. title: The United Nations, Agriculture and the World Economic Revolution.] (789: Aufsätze und Reden, pp. 7—21.) [Cf. 483.]

803 De misdeelde wereld. Strategie tegen de armoede. [Orig. title:] The Challenge of World Poverty. [Samenvatting en uitbouw van Asian Drama.] Vertaald door [Transl. by] E. Marije. Utrecht & Antwerpen, Het Spectrum, 1971, 389 pp. (Spectrum A 5.) [Cf. 739e.]

804 La nécessité de réformes radicales dans les pays en voie de développement. — L'éducation. [Orig. title: The Need for Radical Reforms in Under-Developed Countries. Education.] (Commission internationale sur le développement de l'éducation. Série B: Opinions. 20. Unesco 1971, 12 pp.) [Cf. 806.]
Large extracts of the chapter on education in The Challenge of World Poverty. [Cf. 739a—d.]

805 The Need for Adult Education. (The Peace Corps Volunteer 9: 5—6. 1971, pp. 17—18.)
Article based on The Challenge of World Poverty. [Cf. 739a—d.]

806 The Need for Radical Reforms in Under-Developed Countries. Education. (International Commission on the Development of Education. Series B: Opinions 20. Unesco, 1971, 13 pp.) [Cf. 804.]

807 The Negro Church in the Negro Community. (The Black Church in America. Ed. by Hart M. Nelsen, Raytha L. Yokley [&] Anne K. Nelsen. New York & London 1971, pp. 82—90.)
Repr. from An American Dilemma, pp. 935—942. (127a)

808 The Negro Community as a Pathology (1944). (Blacks in White America Since 1865 . . . [Ed.] by Robert C. Twombly. New York 1971, pp. 496—514.)
From An American Dilemma . . . New York . . . 1969, pp. 928—930, 982—994. [Cf. 697.]

809 Noch einmal: Ein amerikanisches Dilemma. Die Rassenkrise in den Vereinigten Staaten in historischer Perspektive. [Orig. title: The Racial Crisis in Perspective.] (789: Aufsätze und Reden, pp. 106—155.) [Cf. 587.]

810 Objektivität in der Sozialforschung. [Orig. title:] Objectivity in Social Research. Aus dem Amerikanischen von Ursula Deininger. Frankfurt am Main, Suhrkamp, 1971, 117 pp. (Ed. Suhrkamp 508.) [Cf. 712c.]

811 On Economic Theory. (Economic Planning. Structure and Policies 2, September 1971, pp. 20—21.)

812 A Parallel to the Negro Problem. (The Other Minorities. Ed. by Edward Sagarin. Waltham, Mass., & Toronto 1971, pp. 42—50.) [Cf. 1033, 1052.]
Appendix 5 of An American Dilemma. (127a)

813 Paths of Development. Excerpts from . . . New Left Review 36: March—April 1966, pp. 65—74. (Peasants and Peasant Societies . . . Harmondsworth . . . 1971, pp. 412—422.) [Cf. 519.]
Repr. 1973.

814 Political, Social, and Economic Aspects of the Food-Production Problem. (Economic Planning 7 (1971): 3/4, pp. 3—6. — Proceedings SOS/70. Third International Congress [of] Food Science and Technology. Washington, D. C., 1971, pp. 7—11.) [Identical with 752.]

815 The Principle of Circular and Cumulative Causation. (Economic Development and Social Change . . . Ed. by George Dalton. Garden City, N. Y., 1971, pp. 375—385.) [Cf. 263.]

816 Regional Economic Inequalities. (Economic Development and Social Change . . . Ed. by George Dalton. Garden City, N. Y., 1971, pp. 386—400.) [Identical with 252.]

818 Rolle und Realität der Rasse. [Orig. title: The Role and Reality of Race.] (789: Aufsätze und Reden, pp. 82—105.) [Cf. 720.]

819 Saggio sulla povertà di undici paesi asiatici. Una ricerca patrocinata dal Twentieth Century Fund. Trad. a cura di Gaetano Degasperis. [Orig. title:] Asian Drama. An Inquiry into the Poverty of Nations. Principali collaboratori: William J. Barber ... Vol. 1—3. Milano, Il Saggiatore, 1971, pp. I—XXX, 1—699; I—XII, 701—1561; I—XV, 1563—2306. (Biblioteca di studi afroasiatici 1: 1—3.) [Cf. 637, 641f.]

820 Shakai‚kagaku to kachi handan. [Japanese transl. of: Objectivity in Social Research and The Place of Values in Social Policy.] [Transl. by:] Naomi Maruo. Tōkyō, Takeuchi Shoten, 1971, 226 pp. [Cf. 712c, 862.]

821 Stimmt etwas nicht mit dem Wohlfahrtsstaat? [Orig. title: The Swedish Way to Happiness.] (789: Aufsätze und Reden, pp. 40—52.) [Cf. 545.]

822 Ti'ūrī-ji iqtisādī va kišvarhā-ji kam-rušd. [Persian transl. of Economic Theory and Underdeveloped Regions.] [2nd pr.] Tihrān 1349 [= 1971], 224 pp. [Cf. 255e, 525.]

823 To Bring the Atrocities into the Open. Indochina: the US Criminal War. (New Perspectives 1: May 1971: 1, pp. 19—20.)

824 Universitet och högskolor i framtiden. [Universities and University Colleges in the Future.] (Utbildning år 2000. En framtidsstudie av Torsten Husén. Stockholm 1971, pp. 140—143.)

825 Världsnöden. [World Suffering.] [Transl. from the German by Ulrich Herz.] (Alva och Gunnar Myrdal i fredens tjänst. Stockholm, Rabén & Sjögren, 1971, pp. 80—95.) [Cf. 764.]
The German original without title.

826+ Vetenskap och politik i nationalekonomin. [With new Preface.] [With] Appendix: [1:] Efterskrift till Value in Social Theory. [Cf. 299.] [2:] Gustav Cassel in memoriam. [Cf. 155.] [3:] Gustav Cassel. [Cf. 540.] [Ny omarb. uppl. ... Återövers. av Kerstin Lundgren ... av den engelska utgåvan 1953.] [The Political Element in the Development of Economic Theory . . . New, rev. ed. Retransl. of the English ed. 1953 by . . .] Stockholm, Rabén & Sjögren (Tema); Helsingfors, Schildt, 1971, 334 pp. [Cf. 228a.]

Though the book was printed in 1971, this new Swedish edition, like the Preface, bears the year of publication 1972.

827   Vi behöver rebeller. [We Need Rebels.] (Frihet 1971: 4, p. 5.) [Not identical with 356.]

828+   * Vi och Västeuropa. Andra ronden. Uppfordran till eftertanke och debatt. [We and Western Europe. 2nd round. Challenge to Reflection and Discussion.] [With:] Tord Ekström & Roland Pålsson. [Ny, utökad uppl.] [New, enl. ed.] Stockholm, Rabén & Sjögren, 1971, 233 pp. (Tema.) [Cf. 372a.]

829   Vietnam — ein moralisches Problem für die Welt. (606: 12)

830   Der Vietnamkrieg und die politische und moralische Isolierung Amerikas. (532: 36)

831   The War on Poverty. (The Rationale of the Essay. A Reader for Writers. [Ed. by Alice Dhandler & Marlene Fisher.] New York . . . 1971, pp. 371—376.) [Cf. 438, 489.]

832   Warum die Welt von heute nicht heil ist. (Der Mensch und die Technik. Technisch-wissenschaftliche Blätter der Süddeutschen Zeitung 13 (1971) (191. Ausg.): 16. Dezember, p. 1.)

833   What is Wrong with the Welfare State? (European Socialism Since World War I. Ed. . . . by Nathanael Greene. Chicago 1971, pp. 198—207.) [Cf. 968.]

---

834   [Foreword to:] Adler-Karlsson, Gunnar: Der Fehlschlag. Zwanzig Jahre Wirtschaftskrieg zwischen Ost und West. Wien . . . 1971, pp. 7—12.

835   [Foreword to:] Folkmord. Rapport från Internationella kommissionen för undersökning av USA:s krigsförbrytelser i Indokina. [Murder of a Nation. Report of the International

Commission for Investigation into the War Crimes of the U.S.A. in Indo-China.] Red. av [Publ. by] Hans Göran Franck & Tomas Rothpfeffer. Stockholm 1971, pp. 7—9.

836   Det måste finnas en gräns för organisationernas maktspel. [There Must Be a Limit to the Gambling for Power of the Organizations.] (Vår Kyrka 110 (1971): 10, pp. 8—9.)
Svar på frågan: Vart leder [SACO-]strejken? Arbetsmarknad i konflikt. Av Ingmar Stoltz. [Answer to the question: Where Does the Strike Lead to? Labour Market in Conflict.]
Interview.

837   Gunnar Myrdal Talks About Troubles in "Utopia". (Nation's Business 59: 4, April 1971, pp. 44, 48—50.)
Interview in Stockholm in 1971 written by Sterling G. Slappey.

838   "I Have No Respect for Diplomacy in Research." (Ceres 4: 2. 1971, pp. 31—34.) [Cf. 842.]
Interview in March, 1971.

839   * Intervju med Alva och Gunnar Myrdal. Inspelad för Norddeutscher Rundfunk i Genève juli 1970. [Interview with . . . Produced for . . .] (Alva och Gunnar Myrdal i fredens tjänst. Stockholm 1971, pp. 109—146.) [Cf. 825.]
Interview by Ulrich Herz.

840   Interview with Dr. Gunnar Myrdal. (Chronicle, November 13, 1971.) [Identical with 841.]
Interview by Ofield Dukes.

841   Interview with Sweden's Gunnar Myrdal. (The Washington Informer, November 11, 1971.) [Identical with 840.]
Interview by Ofield Dukes.

842   Man dar kare tahghigh ahle molahezeh kari nistam. [Orig. title: I Have No Respect for Diplomacy in Research.] (Negin 1971: November, pp. 5—7, 61.) [Cf. 838.]
Interview in March, 1971. — Title and text in Persian.

843   Styr världen med förnuft — ej med våld! Samtal med Gunnar Myrdal. [Rule the World by Sense — Not by Force! A Dialogue . . .] (Arbetaren 50 (1971): 18, pp. 3, 11.)
Interview by Edvard Ramström.

844 Wettrüsten einstellen. Waffenhandel kontrollieren. (Kontraste 10 (1970/71): 4, pp. 37—39.)
Interview by Reinhold Lehmann about the Stockholm International Peace Research Institute (SIPRI).

1972

845 An American Dilemma — Has It Been Resolved? (Citycorp Magazine 1972: 3—4.) [Cf. 898—899.]

846 American Ideals and the American Conscience. (Nation of Nations. The Ethnic Experience and the Racial Crisis. Ed. by Peter I. Rose. New York ... 1972, pp. 159—164.) [Cf. 276.]

847 Asian Drama. An Inquiry into the Poverty of Nations. An Abridgment by Seth S. King. [Foreword by M. J. Rossant.] New York, Vintage Books, 1972, XIV, 464 pp. (The Twentieth Century Fund.) (A Vintage Book V 730.) [Cf. 641e, 786, 848.]

848 Asian Drama. An Inquiry into the Poverty of Nations. An Abridgement by Seth S. King. [Foreword by M. J. Rossant.] London, Allen Lane The Penguin Press, 1972, X, 388 pp. (The Twentieth Century Fund.) [641d, 786, 847.]

849 Behovet av radikala inhemska reformer. [The Need for Radical Domestic Reforms.] (874: Världsfattigdomen, pp. 36—64.) [Identical with 903. Cf. 859.]
Transl. and adapted from a feature article in the Britannica Book of the Year 1972, pp. 29—34.

850 Conflict of Goals. (The Economic Times 1972, pp. 43, 45.)

851 Economics of an Improved Environment. (The Ad Hoc "Think Tank" and the Ad Hoc Metropolitan Planning Branch of the Diocese of California. Information Paper 36. San Francisco 1972, X, 30 pp. [Stencil.] — Economic Planning 8 (1972): 3/4, pp. 3—15.) [Cf. 910—911, 939, 945.]
Adapted from a lecture ... given in connection with the United Nations Conference on the Human Environment, Stockholm, June 8, 1972.

852 From Sweden. A Program for Americans. (ADA World, April/May 1972, pp. 9—11, 25.)

853 Further Thoughts About An American Dilemma. (Worldview 15 (1972): 12, pp. 29—32.) [Cf. 899.]

854 Growth and Social Justice. (World Development 1 (1972): 3/4, pp. 119—120.) [Cf. 919.]
Article prepared for the Economic Times Annual, Bombay, 1972.

855 How Scientific Are the Social Sciences? (Économies et sociétés 6 (1972), pp. 1473—96. — Journal of Social Issues 28 (1972), pp. 151—170.) [Cf. 925—926, 928.]
The article is based on the first Gordon Allport Memorial Lecture presented at Harvard University, Cambridge, Mass., November 4, 1971.

856 Indiens roll efter kriget. Ur en kommentar. [India's Role after the War. From a Commentary.] (Fogelstad förbundet 29 (1972): 2, pp. 1—2.) [Cf. 919.]
Excerpt from a paper for the Indian press on the Day of the Republic, January 26, 1972. Swedish transl. of the American orig.

857 Indiens Rolle nach seinem Sieg. (Die Zukunft 1972: 9, pp. 10—11.) [Cf. 919.]

858 The Need for a Sociology and Psychology of Social Science and Scientists. (Social Studies. The Humanizing Process. Milton Kleg and John H. Litcher, ed. Winter Haven, Florida, 1972, pp. 1—9.) [Cf. 896a, 942.]
Opening Address, Annual Meeting of the British Sociological Association at the University of York, 11 April, 1972.

860 Om verdensfattigdommen. En skitse for bekæmpelse af fattigdommen i verden. [About World Poverty ...] På dansk ved [Transl. into Danish by] Mogens Boisen. Overs. dels fra svensk efter Politiskt manifest om världsfattigdomen ... og dels fra amerikansk efter The Challenge of World Poverty. København, Fremad, 1972, 466 pp. [Cf. 739e, 760.]

861 On the Necessity for an American Catharsis. ([Foreword to:] The Wasted Nations. Report of the International Commission

of Enquiry into United States Crimes in Indochina, June 20—25, 1971. Ed. by Frank Browning [&] Dorothy Forman. New York . . . & London 1972, pp. VII—X.)

862 The Place of Values in Social Policy. (Institute for International Economic Studies, University of Stockholm. Reprint series 20. [1972], 14 pp. — Journal of Social Policy 1 (1972): 1, pp. 1—14.) [Cf. 820, 896a, 947, 954, 965.]

863+ Political Factors in Economic Assistance. (Scientific American 226: 4. 1972, pp. 15—21.)

864 Politisches Manifest über die Armut in der Welt. [Orig. title:] The Challenge of World Poverty. Aus dem Amerikanischen von Suzanne Reichstein. Gekürzte Ausg. Die Bearb. besorgte Ernst-Josef Pauw. Frankfurt am Main 1972, 286 pp. (Suhrkamp Taschenbuch 40.) [Cf. 739e, 759b.]

865 Population Prospects and Population Policy. (Population Analysis and Studies. Radhakamal Mukerjee commemoration vol. Bombay & New Delhi 1972, pp. 139—154.)

866+ Response to Introduction. (The American Economic Review. Papers and Proceedings . . . 62 (1972), pp. 456—462.) [Cf. 909.]
Response speech at a luncheon for the author and Alva Myrdal given by the American Economic Association on December 28, 1971, in New Orleans.

867 The Social Sciences and Their Impact on Society. (The Rules of the Game. Cross-disciplinary Essays on Models in Scholarly Thought. Ed. by Teodor Shanin. London & New York 1972, pp. 347—359.) [Cf. 667.]
Shortened version.

868 The Sovereignty of Politics. (Worldview 15 (1972): 10, pp. 13—17.)

869 Sovremennye problemy "tret'ego mira". [Drama Azii. Issledovanie niščety narodov.] [Orig. title: Asian Drama. An Inquiry into the Poverty of Nations. Preface by R. A.

114

Ul'janovskij & V. I. Pavlov.] Sokraščennyj perev. s anglijsko-go [Shortened transl. from English] . . . Obščaja red. [Editor-in-Chief] R. A. Ul'janovskogo. Moskva, Izd. Progress, 1972, 768 pp. [Cf. 641f.]

870 The Theory of the Vicious Circle. (The Economics of Black America. Ed. by Harold G. Vatter & Thomas Palm. New York 1972, pp. 9—12.)
Excerpt from An American Dilemma, pp. 75—78. (127a)

871+ Twisted Terminology and Biased Theories. (International Economics and Development. Essays in Honor of Raúl Prebisch. Ed. by Luis Eugenio Di Marco. New York & London 1972, pp. 37—41.) [Identical with 963. Cf. 916, 1000.]

872 Ueber soziale und wirtschaftliche Ungleichheit in Entwicklungsländern. (Neue Wege 66 (1972), pp. 119—122.)

873 De utvecklade ländernas ansvar. [The Responsibility of the Developed Countries.] (874: Världsfattigdomen, pp. 54—63.)

874 Världsfattigdomen. [The World Poverty.] Stockholm, Utrikespolitiska Institutet, 1972, 64 pp. (Världspolitikens dagsfrågor 1972: 6—7.) [Cf. 876, 964, 966.]

875 Were Gandhi to Return. (Worldview 15: 8. 1972, pp. 29—31.)

876 The World Poverty Problem. (Britannica Book of the Year 1972, pp. 22—34. — Poverty, Ecology, and Technological Change: World Problems of Development. Davidson Lectures 1972. Whittemore School of Business and Economics, University of New Hampshire. [1972], pp. 14—27.) [Cf. 874, 929, 970.]

---

877 [Foreword to:] The Effects of Modern Weapons on the Human Environment in Indochina. Documents presented at a hearing organized by the International Commission in cooperation with the Stockholm Conference on Vietnam and the Swedish Committee for Vietnam. Stockholm, June 2—4, 1972. Stockholm [1972], pp. I—II.

878   [Foreword to:] Harvest of Death. Chemical Warfare in Vietnam and Cambodia. [By] J. B. Neilands . . . New York & London 1972, pp. XI—XII.

879   [Foreword to:] The Indochina War in 1972. Reports to the Third Session of the International Commission of Enquiry into U. S. Crimes in Indochina, October 10—16, 1972. Stockholm [1972], pp. 1—2. [Stencil.]
      The session took place in Copenhagen.

880   [Foreword to:] Moberg, Vilhelm: A History of the Swedish People. [Orig. title: Min svenska historia.] Transl. from Swedish by Paul Britten Austin. [P. 1.] New York, 1972, p. [VII].

881   Ett amerikanskt dilemma — har det lösts? [An American Dilemma — Has It Been Resolved?] (Arbetaren 51 (1972): 37, pp. 3, 11.) [Cf. 845, 898.]

882   Bharat ab ek parbavshali desh banhe. [India Should Now Become an Effective and Stable State.] (Amar Ujala 26/1 1972.)
      Title and text in Hindi.

883   Bharat ki vijay uprant bhoomika. [India's History after the Victory.] (Nav Bharat 26/1 1972.) [Cf. 884.]
      Title and text in Hindi.

884   Bharat na vijay pachhi Daxin Asia ma shanti ni shresht tako. [After India's Victory: Definite Opportunity for Peace in South Asia.] (Sandesh 26/1 1972.) [Cf. 883.]
      Title and text in Gujarati.

885   Framsteg och social rättvisa. [Progress and Social Justice.] (Arbetaren 51 (1972): 43, p. 3.)

886   Good-bye to 'Soft State'. (The Tribune 26/1 1972.) [Identical with 887—888.]

887   India Must Say Goodbye to "Soft State". (The Motherland 26/1 1972.) [Identical with 886, 888.]

888 India Should Bid Good-bye to 'Soft State'. (Amrit Bazar Patrika 26/1 1972. — Assam Tribune 26/1 1972.) [Identical with 886—887.]

889 Indien och Bangladesh. (Arbetaren 51 (1972): 13, pp. 9, 11.)

890 The American Dilemma Revisited. America from the Enlightenment Viewpoint. (Current 1972: September, pp. 35—43.) [Cf. 892.]
Interview by Frank L. Keegan.

891 Gunnar Myrdal Comments on: America's Image, Black Rebellion, Limits to Growth and Population Control. (Bulletin of the Atomic Scientists 28 (1972): 9, pp. 5—7.)
Interview by Sally Jacobsen during the United Nations Conference on the Human Environment in Stockholm, June, 1972.

892 Gunnar Myrdal on America's Dilemma: Present and Future. (World 29/8 1972, pp. 29—33.) [Cf. 890.]
Interview by Frank L. Keegan.

893 [The Internationalist's Interview with Gunnar Myrdal.] (The Internationalist 5: March 1972, pp. 22—25.)

894 Is Sweden Richer Than the U. S.? (Forbes 109: 7. 1972, pp. 22—24, 27—28.)
A Forbes interview in Stockholm, 1972.

1973

895 Address at the Inaugural Ceremonies of Professor Woodrow M. Strickler as President of [the University of] Louisville, Kentucky, on November 18th, 1968. (914: Essays and Lectures, pp. 183—197.)

896a+ Against the Stream. Critical Essays on Economics. New York, Pantheon Books, 1973, X, 336 pp.
Contents: Crises and Cycles in the Development of Economics. (909[1]) — "Stagflation". (957) — The Place of Values in Social Policy. (947) — The Need for a Sociology and Psychology of Social Science and Scientists. (942) — The World Poverty Problem. (970) — The Need for Radical Domestic Reforms. (943) — How Scientific Are the Social Sciences? (925)

117

— Twisted Terminology and Biased Ideas. (963) — Politics and Economics in International Relations. (949) — "Growth" and "Development". (922) — Economics of an Improved Environment. (911) — Gandhi as a Radical Liberal. (920) — The Future of India. (919) — Toward a Better America. (961) — An American Dilemma — Has It Been Resolved? (899) — A Brief Note on Marx and "Marxism". (905)

896b — [London] 1974. (980)

896c Translations.
[French:] Procès de la croissance. Paris 1978. (1085)
[German:] Anstelle von Memoiren. Frankfurt am Main 1974. (982)
[Hindi:] Dhārā ke viruddh. Dillī & Patnā 1977. (1066)
[Italian:] Controcorrente. Roma-Bari 1975. (1019)
[Japanese:] Han shuryŭ no keizai-gaku. Tōkyō 1975. (1027)
[Korean:] Kyŏngjehak pip'an. Seoul 1976. (1050)
[Portuguese:] Contra a corrente. Rio de Janeiro 1977. (1065)
[Spanish:] Contra la corriente. Barcelona 1980. (1111)
[Swedish:] I stället för memoarer. Stockholm 1973. (929)

897 Agricultural Development and Planning in the Underdeveloped Countries Outside the Socialist Sphere. National Purpose, Methods, Difficulties and Results. (914: Essays and Lectures, pp. 221—231.) [Cf. 734.]

898 "An American Dilemma" — har det blivit löst? [... Has It Been Resolved?] (929: I stället för memoarer, pp. 296—309.) [Cf. 881, 899.]

899 An American Dilemma — Has It Been Resolved? (896: Against the Stream, pp. 293—307.) [Cf. 898.]
Adapted version of Further Thoughts About An American Dilemma. (853)

900 Asiatisches Drama. Eine Untersuchung über die Armut der Nationen. Eine Studie des Twentieth Century Fund in der Kurzfassung von Seth S. King. [Orig. title: Asian Drama ... Aus dem Englischen von Nils Lindquist.] Frankfurt am Main, Suhrkamp, 1973, 448 pp. [Cf. 641f.]

901 "The Aurangabad Experiment." Programme for Rural Workers Family Welfare. (Free Labor World 1973: December, pp. 17—18.) [Identical with 971.]

118

902 The Beam in Our Eyes. (Comparative Research Methods. Ed. by Donald P. Warwick & Samuel Osherson. Englewood Cliffs, N. J., 1973, pp. 89—99.) [Cf. 329 – 330.]
From Asian Drama . . . Vol. 1. New York, The Twentieth Century Fund, 1968, pp. 16—26. [Cf. 637.]

903 Behovet av inhemska jämlikhetsreformer. [The Need for Domestic Reforms of Equality.] (929: I stället för memoarer, pp. 108 137.) [Identical with 849.]

904 Behovet av sociologiska och psykologiska studier av samhällsforskningen och samhällsforskarna. [The Need for a Sociology and Psychology of Social Science and Scientists.] (929: I stället för memoarer, pp. 61—74.) [Cf. 942.]

905 A Brief Note on Marx and "Marxism". (896a: Against the Stream, pp. 308—316.) [Cf. 934.]

906 Causes and Nature of Development. (Tahqiqāt-e Eqtesādi. Quarterly Journal of Economic Research 10: 29 & 30. 1973, pp. 3—16.) [Stencil.] [Cf. 896a: Against the Stream, particularly Chapters 5, 6 and 10.]

907 Challenge of Stagnation in Developing Countries. (Khadigramodyog 19 (1973), pp. 381—387.) [Identical with 927.] [Cf. 985.]
Opening Address to the Second One Asia Assembly in New Delhi, February 5, 1973.

908+ A Contribution Towards a More Realistic Theory of Economic Growth and Development. — Vers une théorie plus réaliste du développement. — Hacia una teoría más realista del desarrollo. (Mondes en développement 1973, pp. 23—33.) [Cf. 922, 987.]
Text in English.

909¹ Crises and Cycles in the Development of Economics. (896: Against the Stream, pp. 1—16. — Political Quarterly 44 (1973), pp. 9—21.) [Cf. 935.]
Enl. adaptation of Response to Introduction. (866)

909² Il dramma dell'Asia. [Orig. title: Asian drama . . .] Ed. abbreviata del Saggio sulla povertà di undici paesi asiatici a cura di Seth King. Una ricerca patrocinata dal Twentieth Century Fund. Trad. di Lia Volpatti. Vol. 1—2. Milano 1973, 297 pp; 336 pp. (I Grandi Gabbiani 5: 1—2.) [Cf. 637, 641 f.]

910 Economía de un medio ambiente mejorado. [Orig. title: Economics of an Improved Environment.] (Revista del ITCC 1: 2. 1973, pp. 58—75.) [Cf. 911.]

911+ Economics of an Improved Environment. (ITCC Review 2: 2 (6). 1973, pp. 22—39. [Stencil.] — Who Speaks for Earth? Ed. by Maurice F. Strong. New York 1973, pp. 67—105. — World Development 1 (1973), pp. 102—114. — 896: Against the Stream, pp. 197—233.) [Cf. 851.]

912 An Economist's Vision of a Sane World. (914: Essays and Lectures, pp. 87—103.) [Cf. 564.]

913 Equity and Growth. (World Development 1 (1973), pp. 43—47.) [Cf. 991.]
Based on a lecture given in a series celebrating the 20th anniversary of the Banco Nacional do Desenvolvimento Econômico in Rio de Janeiro on 31 August, 1973.

914 Essays and Lectures. [Ed. by Mutsumi Okada. Kyoto, Keibunsha, 1973], 285 pp.
Contents: Inherent Imperfections in Foreign Policy. (932) — The 1965 McDougall Lecture. (495) — What is Wrong with the Welfare State? (968) — Land Reform in Its Broader Economic and Social Setting. (937) — The Social Sciences and Their Impact on Society. (956) — The Vietnam War and the Political and Moral Isolation of America. (532 : 37) — An Economist's Vision of a Sane World. (912) — The Stockholm World Conference on Vietnam. (959) — The Necessity and Difficulty of Planning the Future Society. (941) — Political Factors Affecting East-West Trade in Europe. (948) — Twenty Years of the United Nations Economic Commission for Europe. (962) — Gandhi as a Radical Liberal. (920) — The Role and Reality of Race. (953) — Address at the Inaugural Ceremonies of Professor Woodrow M. Strickler as President of [the University of] Louisville, 1968. (895) — The Role of the Public Services in Underdeveloped Countries. (955) — Biases in Social Research. (737) — Agricultural Development and Planning in the Underdeveloped Countries Outside the Socialist Sphere. National Purpose, Methods, Difficulties and Results. (897) — Address delivered at the Inaugural Meeting of the One Asia Assembly . . . 1970. (732) — India's Development: An Evaluation. (930) — The Intergovernmental Organizations and the Role of their Secretariats. (933)

915 Exalt the Inherited Ideals. Justice, Liberty, Equality, Brotherhood. (Going-to-College Handbook 27 (1973), pp. 10—12.)

916 Förvanskad terminologi och skeva föreställningar. [Twisted Terminology and Biased Ideas.] (929: I stället för memoarer, pp. 164—172.) [Cf. 871, 963.]

917 Free Trade and Inequality. From Rich Lands and Poor, 1957 . . . (Perspectives on the Economic Problem. A Book of Readings in Political Economy. Ed. by Arthur MacEwan and Thomas E. Weisskopf. 2nd ed. Englewood Cliffs, N.J., 1973, pp. 287—291.) [Cf. 265, 747.]

918 The Full Meaning of More Food. (Asian Trade & Industry 5: 7. 1973, pp. 27—28.)
Anonymous.

919 The Future of India. (896a: Against the Stream, pp. 245—264.) [Cf. 931.]
Adapted from two articles: "India's New Role Following Victory", published in the Indian press for Republic Day, January 26, 1972, and "Growth and Social Justice", in The Economic Times Annual, October 1972 . . . [Cf. 882—884.]

920 Gandhi as a Radical Liberal. (896a: Against the Stream, pp. 234—244. — 914: Essays and Lectures, pp. 153—161.) [Cf. 653, 704.]

921 Gandhi som liberal radikal [!]. [Orig. title: Gandhi as a Radical Liberal.] (929: I stället för memoarer, pp. 239—249.) [Cf. 920.]

922 "Growth" and "Development". (896a: Against the Stream, pp. 182—196.) [Cf. 908, 960.]

923 Growth: Gross and Net. (Social Policy 4: 3. November/December 1973, pp. 22—26.)
Excerpted from Against the Stream: "Growth" and "Development", pp. 182—196. [Cf. 896a, 922.]

924 Grundprobleme der unterentwickelten Länder. [Title of the orig. ms.: The Main Problems of Development in Underdeveloped Countries.] [Die deutsche Übers. wurde von Mitgliedern der Fachgruppe Makroökonomie der Universität Augsburg vorgenommen.] Augsburg, Die Brigg, [1973?], 25 pp. (Volkswirtschaftliche Vortragsreihe.)
Lecture given in the Rathaus of Augsburg, 8 June, 1971.

925 How Scientific Are the Social Sciences? (Bulletin of the Atomic Scientists 29 (1973): 1, pp. 31—37. — 896a: Against the Stream, pp. 133—157.) [Cf. 855, 926, 928.]

926 [How Scientific Are the Social Sciences?] Rejoinder [to Comment on "How Scientific Are the Social Sciences?" [By] D. Stuart Conger]. (Journal of Social Issues 29 (1973): 2, pp. 215—218.) [Cf. 855, 925.]

927 Human Dimensions of Economic Growth. (The States 4: 8. 1973, pp. 9—10, 17, 19.) [Identical with 907.]
Opening Address to the Second One Asia Assembly, New Delhi, February 5, 1973.

928 Hur vetenskapliga är samhällsvetenskaperna? [How Scientific Are the Social Sciences?] (929: I stället för memoarer, pp. 138—163.) [Cf. 925.]

929 I stället för memoarer. Kritiska essäer om nationalekonomin. [Orig. title: Against the Stream. Critical Essays on Economics.] Till svenska av [Transl. by] Anders Byttner och Kerstin Lundgren. Stockholm, Prisma, 1973, 324 pp. [Cf. 896c.]
Contents: Kriser och cykler i nationalekonomins utveckling. (935) — "Stagflation". (958) — "Värdenas" roll i socialpolitiken. (965) — Behovet av sociologiska och psykologiska studier av samhällsforskningen och samhällsforskarna. (904) — Världsfattigdomens problem. (966) — Behovet av inhemska jämlikhetsreformer. (903) — Hur vetenskapliga är samhällsvetenskaperna? (928) — Förvanskad terminologi och skeva föreställningar. (916) — Politik och ekonomi i internationella sammanhang. (950) — "Tillväxt" och "utveckling". (960) — Miljöförbättringens ekonomi. (939) — Gandhi som liberal radikal. (921) — Indiens framtid. (931) — Mot ett bättre Amerika. (940) — "An American Dilemma" — har det blivit löst? (898) — Korta anmärkningar om Marx och "marxismen". (934)

930 India's Development: An Evaluation. Gunnar Myrdal's Foreword to Tarlok Singh's book [India's Development Experience]. (914: Essays and Lectures, pp. 241—246.) [Cf. 1005.]

931 Indiens framtid. [The Future of India.] (929: I stället för memoarer, pp. 250—269.) [Cf. 919.]

932 Inherent Imperfections in Foreign Policy. (914: Essays and Lectures, pp. 1—10.) [Cf. 465.]

933 The Intergovernmental Organizations and the Role of their Secretariats. (914: Essays and Lectures, pp. 247—270.) [Cf. 705.]

934 Korta anmärkningar om Marx och "marxismen". [A Brief Note on Marx and "Marxism".] (929: I stället för memoarer, pp. 310—318.) [Cf. 905.]

935 Kriser och cykler i nationalekonomins utveckling. [Crises and Cycles in the Development of Economics.] (929: I stället för memoarer, pp. 13—28.) [Cf. 909¹.]

936 Kritischer Realismus in der Bruttosozialprodukt-Rechnung. (G[ottlieb]D[uttweiler]I[nstitut] Topics 4 (1973): 1, pp. 55—62.)

937 Land Reform in Its Broader Economic and Social Setting. (914: Essays and Lectures, pp. 39—53.) [Cf. 509.]

938 Limits to the Limits to Growth. (Unesco Courier 26 (1973): January, pp. 12—13.)
Excerpt from a major address delivered as a part of the Distinguished Lecture Series in Stockholm [1972]. — Transl. into several languages.

939 Miljöförbättringens ekonomi. [Economics of an Improved Environment.] (929: I stället för memoarer, pp. 202—238.) [Cf. 911.]

940 Mot ett bättre Amerika. [Toward a Better America.] (929: I stället för memoarer, pp. 270—295.) [Cf. 961.]

941 The Necessity and Difficulty of Planning the Future Society. (914: Essays and Lectures, pp. 115—126.) [Cf. 661.]

942 The Need for a Sociology and Psychology of Social Science and Scientists. (914: Against the Stream, pp. 52—64. — World Development 1 (1973), pp. 41—46.) [Cf. 858, 896a, 904.]

943 The Need for Radical Domestic Reforms. (896a: Against the Stream, pp. 101—132.)
Adapted from a feature article in the Britannica Book of the Year 1972, pp. 29—34. [Cf. 876.]

944 L'obiettività nelle scienze sociali. L'illusione della "neutralità" della scienza. [Orig. title: Objectivity in Social Research.] [Trad. di Alessandro Casiccia.] Torino, Giulio Einaudi, 1973, 88 pp. (Novo Politecnico 59.) [Cf. 712c.]

945 Ökonomie der verbesserten Umwelt — Strategien wider die Selbstmordgesellschaft. [Orig. title: Economics of an Improved Environment.] Übers. von Henrich von Nussbaum u. Manfred Müller. (Die Zukunft des Wachstums ... Hrsg. [von] Henrich von Nussbaum. Düsseldorf 1973, pp. 13—44.) [Cf. 851.]

946 Pannattu Poruladharam. [Orig. title:] An International Economy. Problems and Prospects. Transl. [into Tamil] by T. C. Mohan. New Delhi (pr. in Madras), The Tamil Nadu Text Society, 1973, 402 pp. [Cf. 244d.]

947 The Place of Values in Social Policy. (896a: Against the Stream, pp. 33—51.) [Cf. 862.]

948 Political Factors Affecting East-West Trade in Europe. (914: Essays and Lectures, pp. 127—138.) [Identical with 665, 716.]

949 Politics and Economics in International Relations. (896a: Against the Stream, pp. 167—181.) [Cf. 950.]
Adapted from an unpublished lecture at the 14th International Seminar for Diplomats, Schloss Klesheim bei Salzburg, July 30, 1971.

950 Politik och ekonomi i internationella sammanhang. [Orig. title: Politics and Economics in International Relations.] (929: I stället för memoarer, pp. 173—186.) [Cf. 949.]

951 The Relentless Drive Toward Egalitarianism. (Business and Society Review, Autumn 1973: 7, pp. 14—19.)
The article is adapted from the author's forthcoming book Against the Stream. (896)

952 Reto a la pobreza. [Orig. title:] The Challenge of World Poverty. Presentación: Francis O. Wilcox. Trad. castellana de Santiago Udina. Barcelona, Ariel, 1973, 571 pp. (Colección Demos.) [Cf. 739e.]

953 The Role and Reality of Race. (914: Essays and Lectures, pp. 163—181.) [Cf. 720.]

954 Rôle des valeurs et politique sociale. [Orig. title: The Place of Values in Social Policy.] Trad. de l'anglais par Mme Pineau-Valenciennes. (Consommation 20 (1973), pp. 5—16.) [Cf. 862.]

955 The Role of the Public Services in Underdeveloped Countries. (914: Essays and Lectures, pp. 199—209.) [Cf. 721.]

956 The Social Sciences and Their Impact on Society. (914: Essays and Lectures, pp. 55—71.) [Cf. 667.]
On the occasion of the Fifteenth Anniversary Celebration of the School of Applied Social Sciences, Western Reserve University, Cleveland, Ohio, September 29—October 1, 1966.

957 "Stagflation." (896a: Against the Stream, pp. 29—43.) [Cf. 958.]
English text.

958 "Stagflation." (929: I stället för memoarer, pp. 29—43.) [Cf. 957.]
Swedish text.

959 The Stockholm World Conference on Vietnam. (914: Essays and Lectures, pp. 105—114.)
Closing Address at the Stockholm World Conference on Vietnam, July 9, 1967, including the author's article "Vietnam — a Moral Problem for the Whole World". (606)

960 "Tillväxt" och "utveckling". ["Growth" and "Development".] (929: I stället för memoarer, pp. 187—201.) [Cf. 922.]

961 Toward a Better America. (896a: Against the Stream, pp. 266—292.) [Cf. 940.]

962 Twenty Years of the United Nations Economic Commission for Europe. (914: Essays and Lectures, pp. 139—152.) [Cf. 673.]

963 Twisted Terminology and Biased Ideas. (896a: Against the Stream, pp. 158—166.) [Cf. 916.]
Adapted from an essay [Twisted Terminology and Biased Theories] in International Economics and Development...

964 Ulighed og underudvikling. [Inequality and Underdevelopment.] Overs. og red. [Transl. and ed.]: Niels Viderø. København, Mellemfolkeligt samvirke, 1973, 63 pp.
Rev. ed. of the Swedish orig. "Världsfattigdomen". (874)

965 "Värdenas" roll i socialpolitiken. [The Place of Values in Social Policy.] (929: I stället för memoarer, pp. 44—60.) [Cf. 862.]

966 Världsfattigdomens problem. [The World Poverty Problem.] (929: I stället för memoarer, pp. 75—107.) [Cf. 874.]

967 The Vietnam War and the Political and Moral Isolation of America. (914: Essays and Lectures, pp. 73—86.) [Cf. 532: 37.]

968 What is Wrong with the Welfare State? (914: Essays and Lectures, pp. 27—37.) [Cf. 833.]

969 Women: A Parallel to the Negro Problem. (Spectrum on Social Problems. Society, Economy, and Man. Ed. by Jon M. Shepard. Columbus, Ohio, 1973, pp. 181—187.)
From An American Dilemma. New York 1944, pp. 1073—1078. (127a)

970 The World Poverty Problem. (The Britannica Book of the Year 1972, pp. 22—34. — Mondes en développement 1. 1973, pp. 117—161. — 896a: Against the Stream, pp. 65—100.) [Cf. 876.]

---

971 [Foreword to:] The Aurangabad Experiment. Programme for Rural Workers Family Welfare. [New Delhi 1973], 2 pp. [Identical with 901.]

972 [Foreword to:] Elmandjra, Mahdi: The United Nations System. An Analysis. London 1973, pp. 13—14.)

973 [Introduction to:] Adler-Karlsson, Gunnar: Funktionaler Sozialismus. Ein schwedisches Glaubensbekenntnis zur modernen Demokratie. Aus dem Schwedischen von Christina Kossmann. Zug 1973, pp. 9—27. [Cf. 974, 1039.]

974 [Introduction to:] Adler-Karlsson, Gunnar: Funktions-socialisme. Alternativet mellem kommunisme og kapitalisme. Paa dansk ved Annelise Malmgren. [Indledning af Gunnar Myrdal.] København 1973, pp. 9—25.) [Cf. 973.]

975 People — as Well as Money — Build a Nation. (Himmat. Asia's Voice, April 13, 1973.)
From an address to the One Asia Assembly in New Delhi in February, 1973.

976 Gespräch mit Gunnar Myrdal. (Frau und Frieden 22 (1973): Oktober, pp. 3, 6.)
Interview by Alma Kettig.

977 [Gesprek over het rapport van de Club van Rome.] (Grenzen aan de groei. 75 gesprekken over het rapport van de Club van Rome. [Ed. by] Willem L. Oltmans. Vertaling [Transl.]: C. M. Bouman ... Utrecht & Antwerpen 1973, pp. 240—245.) [Cf. 1010.]
Interview.

978 The Islamabad Drama. (Pakistan Economist, May 19—25. 1973, pp. 14—17.)
Interview.

979 Watergate Aftermath ... Gunnar Myrdal's Therapy to Heal America's Psyche. (Today's Health, August 1973, pp. 16, 19, 63—64.)
Interview by Jim Atwater.

1974

980 Against the Stream. Critical Essays on Economics. [London], Macmillan, 1974, X, 336 pp. [Cf. 896a—b.]

981 Ajia no dorama. Shokokumin no hinkon no ichi kenkyū. [Japanese transl. of: Asian Drama. An Inquiry into the Poverty of Nations. An Abridgment by Seth S. King.] Chief

of compilation: Yoichi Itagaki. Joint transl.: Takashi Konami and Shuzo Kimura. 1—2. Tōkyō, Toyo Keizai Shimpo Sha, 1974, 252 pp.; pp. I—VI, 253—559. [Cf. 641f, 786.]

982 Anstelle von Memoiren. Kritische Studien zur Ökonomie. [Orig. title:] Against the Stream. Critical Essays on Economics.] Aus dem Englischen und Amerikanischen von Brigitte Stein. Frankfurt [am Main], Suhrkamp, 1974, 323 pp. [Cf. 896c.]

983 The Case Against Romantic Ethnicity. (The Center Magazine 7 (1974): 4, pp. 26—30.) [Cf. 999.]
With Response to Gunnar Myrdal by Michael Novak. — The article has been widely reproduced in the daily press, for example in the Chicago Tribune, July 21, 1974.

984 Causas y naturaleza del desarrollo. [Con] Preguntas y respuestas. — Causes and Nature of Development. [With] Questions and answers. Caracas 1974, 63 pp.
Lecture in the Central Bank of Venezuela, September 3, 1973. — Spanish and English text.

985+ Challenge of Stagnation in Developing Countries. (Journal of Gandhian Studies, July 1974.) [Cf. 907.]

986 Che cos' è lo sviluppo? [Orig. title: What Is Development?] (Economia pubblica 4 (1974): 10, pp. 3—6.) [Cf. 1003.]

987 Contribución a una teoría más realista del crecimiento y el desarrollo económicos. [Transl. by Eduardo L. Suárez.] (El trimestre económico 41 (1974), pp. 217—229.) [Cf. 908.]

988 First We Must Change Society. (The Bulletin of the Atomic Scientists 30 (1974): 6, pp. 36—37.)

989+ Friedensforschung und die Friedensbewegung. (Anstoss und Ermutigung. Gustav W. Heinemann Bundespräsident 1969—1974. Hrsg. von Heinrich Böll ... Frankfurt am Main 1974, pp. 135, 137—151.)
Transl. and enl. issue of Peace Research and the Peace Movements. [Cf. 997[1].]

990 Human Values in the Economic Equation. (Economic Impact 1974: 7, pp. 56—60.)
Adapted from Against the Stream. [Cf. 896a]

991 Justiça Social e Desenvolvimento. [Orig. title: Equity and Growth.] (Painéis internacionais sobre desenvolvimento socio-econômico. Rio de Janeiro & São Paulo 1974, pp. 359—376 [incl. discussion].) [Cf. 913.]

992 Korruptionen — dess orsaker och verkningar. [Orig. title: Corruption — Its Causes and Effects.] (Utvecklingsekonomi 2. Planering och resursmobilisering. Urval och kommentarer av Mats Lundahl och Bo Södersten. Stockholm 1974, pp. 257—278.)
Swedish transl. of chapter 20 of Asian Drama. (637)

993 Korunk kihīvása: a világszegénység. Egy szegénység elleni világprogram vázlata. [Orig. title:] The Challenge of World Poverty. A World Anti-Poverty Program in Outline. Fordí-totta [Transl. by] Félix Pál. A fordítást ellenőrizte [Transl. rev. by] Berendt T. Iván. Az utószót írta [Concluding Re-mark]: Bognár József. Budapest, Gondolat, 1974, 633 pp. (Társadalomtudományi könyvtár.) [Cf. 739e.]

994 Das logische Kreuz aller Wissenschaft. [Orig. title: The Logical Crux of All Science.] (996: Ökonomische Theorie und unterentwickelte Regionen, pp. 148—152.) [Cf. 258, 308.]

995+ Mass Passivity in America. (The Center Magazine 7 (1974): 2, pp. 72—75.)

996 Ökonomische Theorie und unterentwickelte Regionen. — Weltproblem Armut. [Orig. titles: Economic Theory and Under-Developed Regions. — The World Poverty Problem.] Mit einem Vorwort von Gunnar Adler-Karlsson. Aus dem Englischen übertr. von Ben Lehbert. Frankfurt am Main, Fischer Taschenbuch Verlag, 1974, 199 pp. [Cf. 255e, 876.]

997¹ Peace Research and the Peace Movements. (Center Report 7 (1974): 3, pp. 5—6.) [Cf. 989.]

997² La pobreza de las naciones. Ed. abreviada a cargo de Seth S. King para The Twentieth Century Fund. [Orig. title:] Asian

Drama . . . An abridgment by . . . Trad. castellana de Joaquim Sempere. Ariel, Esplugues de Llobregat, Barcelona 1974, 536 pp. (Demos. Biblioteca de ciencia económica.) [Cf. 641f.]

998+ The Population Problem of Underdeveloped Countries. Paper . . . (Bulletin of the Atomic Scientists special issue in June, 1974, on population, 6 pp.)

999 Reply [to Francis H. Eterovich's remarks on Myrdal's article: The Case Against Romantic Ethnicity]. (The Center Magazine 7 (1974): 6, p. 79.) [Cf. 983.]

1000 Terminología equívoca y teorías sesgadas. [Orig. title: Twisted Terminology and Biased Theories.] (Economía internacional y desarrollo. Estudios en honor de Raúl Prebisch. Buenos Aires 1974, pp. 39—43.) [Cf. 871.]

1001 The Transfer of Technology to Underdeveloped Countries. (Scientific American, September 1974, pp. 173—178, 180, 182. — The Human Population. A Scientific American Book. San Francisco 1974, pp. 129—137.) [Cf. 1035.]

1002 Weltproblem Armut. [Orig. title: The World Poverty Problem.] (996: Ökonomische Theorie und unterentwickelte Regionen, pp. 153—192.)

1003+ What Is Development? (Journal of Economic Issues 8 (1974): pp. 729—736.) [Cf. 986, 1037.]
This volume of the Journal of Economic Issues was published in commemoration of the work of Professor Clarence E. Ayres.

1004 The White Man's Theory of Color Caste. (Readings in Sociology. Ed. by Edgar A. Schuler . . . 5th ed. New York 1974, pp. 321—328.)
From An American Dilemma, pp. 57—67. (127a.)

––––––––––

1005 [Foreword to:] Singh, Tarlok: India's Development Experience. Delhi . . . 1974, pp. VII—XI. [Cf. 930.]

1006 Vad är utveckling? [What Is Development?] (Arbetaren 53 (1974): 42, pp. 6—7.)

1007 Därför reser Gunnar Myrdal tillbaka till USA: Doktorn måste ägna sig åt de allvarligt sjuka . . . [That's Why Gunnar Myrdal Goes Back to U.S.A.: The Doctor Must Devote Himself to the Seriously Ill.] (Aftonbladet 29/9 1974.)
Interview by Lars Weiss.

1008 "Det här var kul, förbannat kul!" ["This Is Nice, Damned Nice!"] (Aftonbladet 10/10 1974.)
Interview in New York with Gunnar Myrdal when he was awarded the Prize for Economic Science in memory of Alfred Nobel. — Interview by Rolf Svensson.

1009 Gunnar Myrdal i Kalifornien: Det finaste med vårt nya liv här — att jag får vara 24 timmar om dygnet med Alva. [G. M. in California: The Best with Our New Life Here — Now I Can Be with Alva Throughout the 24 Hours . . .] (VeckoJournalen 1974: 25, pp. 4—5, 45.)
Interview by Viveka Vogel.

1010 [Interview mit] Gunnar Myrdal. [Aus dem Holländischen übers. von Roland Fleissner.] (Die Grenzen des Wachstums. Pro et Contra. [Hrsg. von Willem L. Oltmans.] Reinbek bei Hamburg 1974, pp. 33—39.) [Cf. 977.]

1011 "Kärvare politik krävs. Revalvera, sänk momsen." ["A More Rigorous Policy Is Necessary. Revalue, Lower the Moms" [= the Value Added Tax].] (Svenska Dagbladet 16/12 1974.)
Talk between Gunnar Myrdal and Nils Lundgren. Text by Kjell Pettersson.

1012 Myrdal med mera. Dialog-telefonsamtal Gunnar Myrdal, Santa Barbara (Californien), och Andreas Ådahl, Stockholm/Uppsala. [Myrdal, etc. Telephone Conversation Between . . .] (Ekonomen 1974: 7, p. 6.)
Interview.

1013 Standstill in South Asia. (Challenge 1974: January/ February, pp. 30—34.)
Interview.

1014 "This Economic Nonsense Must Stop." (Newsweek October 28, 1974, p. 56.)
Interview by Patricia J. Sethi.

1015[1] Against the Stream. Critical Essays on Economics. New York, Vintage, 1975, 336 pp. [Cf. 896a.]

1015[2] Aišian drāma. Qaumon ke iflās kā ğā'iza. [Orig. title:] Asian Drama. [An Inquiry into the Poverty of Nations.] Abridgement by Seth S. King. Urdu transl. by the Economic Research Dept., National Bank of Pakistan, supervision [by] Jamiluddin Aali. Karachi, 1975, 480 pp. [Cf. 641f.]

1015[3] An American Dilemma. The Negro Problem and Modern Democracy. With the assistance of Richard Sterner and Arnold Rose. Vol. 1—2. New York, Pantheon Books, [1975], pp. I—LXXXI, 1—520, 1181—1335, 1441—1484; I—XII, 521—1180, 1335[!]—1485. [Cf. 127e.]
New paperback ed. — As to pagination, see footnote on p. XVII, Vol. 1.

1016 Ceylon and South-East Asia. (Asiyanu Sanwardanaye Desapalanaya. [The Politics of Development in Asia.] Sri Lanka 1975.)
From Asian Drama. Chapter 9. (637) — Title and text in Singhalese.

1017 Coming of Independence. (Yatath Wijithawadaya Saha Sanwardanaya. [Colonialism and Development.] P. 1. Sri Lanka 1975.)
From Asian Drama, pp. 131—147. (637) — Title and text in Singhalese.

1018 Concepts and Practice of Socialism. (Asiyanu Sanwardanaye Desapalanaya. [The Politics of Development in Asia.] Sri Lanka 1975.)
From Asian Drama. Chapter 17. (637) — Title and text in Singhalese.

1019 Controcorrente. Realtà di oggi e teorie di ieri. [Italian transl. of:] Against the Stream. Critical Essays on Economics. Trad. di Bruno Maffi. Roma-Bari, Gius. Laterza & Figli Spa, 1975, 260 pp. (Libri del Tempo Laterza. 148.) [Cf. 896c.]

1020 The Economic Impact of Colonialism. (Yatath Wijithawadaya Saha Sanwardanaya. [Colonialism and Development.] P. 2. Sri Lanka 1975.)
From Developing the Underdeveloped Countries. Ed. by Alan B. Mountjoy. London . . . 1971, pp. 52—57. (793[1]) — Title and text in Singhalese.

1021 Economic Nationalism in the Under-Developed Countries. (Sanwardanaye Desapalana Gathika Swabhawaya. [Political Dynamics and Development.] Sri Lanka 1975.)

From Beyond the Welfare State. Chapter 12. (322) — Title and text in Singhalese.

1022 Economic Planning in the Other Two Orbits. (Sanwardanaye Desapalana Gathika Swabhawaya. [Political Dynamics and Development.] Sri Lanka 1975.)

From Beyond the Welfare State. Chapter 8. (322) — Title and text in Singhalese.

1023 Educational Reform in Underdeveloped Countries. (Proceedings of the 1974 ETS Invitational Conference, [pr. 1975], pp. 45—53.)

Luncheon Address at the 35th ETS Invitational Conference ... held at the New York Hilton, New York City, on November 2, 1974.

1024 Equality and Democracy. (Asiyanu Sanwardanaye Desapalanaya. [The Politics of Development in Asia.] Sri Lanka 1975.)

From Asian Drama. Chapter 16. (637) — Title and text in Singhalese.

1025 The Equality Issue in World Development. (Les Prix Nobel en 1974. Stockholm 1975, pp. 263—281. — Institute for International Economic Studies, University of Stockholm. Reprint series 47. 1975. — Repr. from The Swedish Journal of Economics 77 (1975), pp. 413—432.) [Cf. 1029.]

Nobel Memorial Lecture, The Stockholm School of Economics, March 17, 1975.

1026 Frontiers of Independence. (Yatath Wijithawadaya Saha Sanwardanaya. [Colonialism and Development.] P. 1. Sri Lanka 1975.

From Asian Drama, pp. 175—189. (637) — Title and text in Singhalese.

1027 Han shuryŭ no keizai-gaku. [Orig. title: Against the Stream.] Transl. by Hiroshi Katō and Naomi Maruo. Tōkyō, Diamond Gendai Sensho, 1975, 296 pp. [Cf. 896c.]

1028 Is Social Reform Productive? (The Alumni Association of the Columbia University School of Social Work. Newsletter, Summer 1975, p. 1.)

1029 Jämlikhetsfrågan i världsutvecklingen. [Orig. title: The Equality Issue in World Development.] (Documenta. Kungl. Vetenskapsakademien. 19. 1975, 12 pp.) [Cf. 1025.]

1030 The Meaning and Validity of Institutional Economics.

(Economics in the Future. Ed. by Kurt Dopfer. London, Macmillan, 1976, pp. 82—89.) [Cf. 1069.]

1031 "New Economic Order? Humbug!" (Sweden Now 9 (1975): 4, pp. 24—27.)
Excerpts from the author's Nobel lecture, 1975. (1025)

1032 On Reforming Economic Aid. (Center Report 8 (1975): 1, pp. 3—5.)

1033 A Parallel to the Negro Problem. (Readings and Conversations in Social Psychology. Psychology Is Social. [Ed. by] Edward Krupat. Glenview, Ill., ... 1975, pp. 56—59.) [Cf. 812, 1052.]
Appendix 5 of An American Dilemma. (127a)

1034 Przeciw nędzy na świecie. Zarys światowego programu walki z nędzą. Słowem wstępnym opatrżył Zygmunt Szymański. Przełożył Wojciech Adamiecki. [Orig. title:] The Challenge of World Poverty. A World Anti-Poverty Program in Outline. Introd. by ... Transl. by ... Warszawa, Państwowy Instytut Wydawniczy, 1975, 515 pp. (Biblioteka myśli współczesnej.) [Cf. 739e.]

1035 Le transfert de technologies vers les pays en voie de développement. [Orig. title: The Transfer of Technology to Underdeveloped Countries.] Trad. par Bernard Cazes. (Économie & humanisme 225 (sept./oct. 1975).) [Cf. 1001.]

1036[1] The Unity of the Social Sciences. (Human Organization 34 (1975): 4.)
Plenary Address to the Society for Applied Anthropology, Amsterdam, March 21, 1975.

1036[2] Das Wertproblem in der Sozialwissenschaft. [Orig. title: Value in Social Theory.] Mit einer Einführung und einem Anhang von Paul Streeten. Die Übers. besorgten (mit Ausnahme der Kapitel 1, 10 und 11) Suzanne Reichstein und Manfred Schüler. 2. Aufl. Bonn-Bad Godesberg, Neue Gesellschaft, 1975, 274 pp. (Schriftenreihe des Forschungsinstituts der Friedrich-Ebert-Stiftung 40.) [Cf. 491.]

1037 What Is Development? (Ekistics 40: 237, August 1975, pp. 84—87.) [Cf. 1003.]

1038 What Is Political Economy? (Papers in Economic Criticism.

Published in Commemoration of the First Frank E. Seidman Distinguished Award in Political Economy. [Ed. by] Memphis State University, May 1975, pp. 3—8.)

1039 [Introduction to:] Adler-Karlsson, Gunnar: El socialismo funcional en Suecia. La teoría sueca para una socialización democrática. [Orig. title:] Funktionaler Sozialismus ... Prólogo por Gunnar Myrdal. Versión castellana de Cristobal Piechocki. Buenos Aires [1975], pp. 11—27. (Paidos 77.) [Cf. 973.]

1976

1040 An American Dilemma. (Race and Ethnic Relations. Sociological Readings. Ed. by Gordon Bowker [and] John Carrier. London, Hutchinson, 1976. pp. 37—39.)
Extracts from An American Dilemma, pp. lxxi—lxxiii, lxxiv—lxxv. (127a)

1041 Asia-ŭi tŭrama. Chŏ kungmin-ŭi pin'gon-e kwanhan yŏn'gu. [Orig. title:] Asian Drama. An Inquiry Into the Poverty of Nations. An Abridgement by Seth S. King. [Korean transl. by] Ch'oe Kwang-nyŏl. Seoul, Hyŏnam sa, 1976, 486 pp. [Cf. 641f.]
Repr. 1977, 1980.

1042 A Brief Note on Marx and 'Marxism'. (Readings in Political Economy. Vol. 1. Ed. by E. L. Wheelwright and Frank J. B. Stilwell. Sydney, Australia and New Zealand Book Co., 1976, pp. 266—71.) [Cf. 896a, 905.]
From Against the Stream, London, Macmillan, 1974.

1043 Crises and Cycles in the Development of Economics. (Readings in Political Economy. Vol. 1. Ed. by E. L. Wheelwright and Frank J. B. Stilwell. Sydney, Australia and New Zealand Book Co., 1976, pp. 222—28.) [Cf. 896a, 909[1].]
From Against the Stream, New York, Vintage, 1975.

1044 Crisi e cicli nello sviluppo della scienza economica. [Orig. title: Crises and Cycles in the Development of Economics.] (Il disagio degli economisti. A cura di Riccardo Fiorito.

Trad. di Rita Pasqualini e Joseph Halevi. Firenze, La Nuova Italia, 1976, pp. 85—99. Dimensioni 37.) [Cf. 909[1].]
From The Political Quarterly 44 (1973):1.

1045 Le drame de l'Asie. Une enquête sur la pauvreté des nations. Une étude de la fondation du XXe siècle condensé par Seth King, traduite de l'anglais par Michel Janin. Titre original: Asian Drama. An Inquiry Into the Poverty of Nations. Paris, Seuil, 1976, 411 pp. (Collections esprit.) [Cf. 641f.]

1046 El elemento político en el desarrollo de la teoría económica. [Orig. title:] The Political Element in the Development of Economic Theory . . . Madrid, Gredos, 1976. [Cf. 233, 565.]

1047 Environment and Economic Growth. (IIES. Seminar Paper. No. 57, 1976, 50 pp.) [Cf. 1049, 1051.]
Commemorative lecture at the International Symposium sponsored by The Nihon Keizai Shimbun and the Japan Productivity Center, May 26, 1976, in Tokyo, Japan.

1048 Fukushi kokka to keizai seichō. [Orig. title:] The Welfare State and Economic Growth. [Japanese transl. by] Kondō Masaomi. (Kōken Kanagawa, No. 59, 1976, pp. 4—15, 30—42.) Tokushū: Myurudāru kyōju kōenkai. [Special issue devoted to Myrdal's lecture.])
English and Japanese text.

1049 Kankyō to keizai seichō. [Orig. title: Environment and Economic Growth.] Kinen kōen, Nihon keizai shimbun-sha, Nihon seisan sei honbu, kyōsai kokusai shimpojiumu. [Commemorative lecture, . . . International Symposium.] 26.5.1976. Tokyo, 1976, 19 pp. [Cf. 1047, 1051.]

1050 Kyŏngjehak pip'an. (Wanyŏk: Pan churyu kyŏngjehak.) [Orig. title:] Against the Stream. Critical Essays on Economics. [Korean transl. by] Ch'oe Kwang-nyŏl. Seoul, Hyŏnam sa, 1976, 430 pp. (Hyŏnam sinsŏ 40.) [Cf. 896c.]
Repr. 1978.

1051 Miljö och ekonomisk tillväxt. [Orig. title:] Environment and Economic Growth. Transl. into Swedish [from the author's English MS] by Sam Eckerbom. Stockholm, Utrikespolitiska Institutet, 1976, 48 pp. (Världspolitikens dagsfrågor 1976: 8—9.) [Cf. 1047.]

1052 A Parallel to the Negro Problem. (The Borzoi College Reader. By Charles Muscatine & Marlene Griffith. 3rd ed. New York, 1976, pp. 380 ff.) [Cf. 812, 1033.]
Appendix 5 of An American Dilemma. (127a) — 1st ed. 1966, 2nd ed. 1971.

1053 Das politische Element in der nationalökonomischen Doktrinbildung. [Orig. title: Vetenskap och politik i nationalekonomien.] Mit einem Vorwort von Paul Streeten. Übers. . . . anhand der englischen Ausgabe durch M. Schüler bearb. 2. Aufl. Bonn-Bad Godesberg, Verlag Neue Gesellschaft, 1976, 210 pp. (Schriftreihe des Forschungsinstituts der Friedrich-Ebert-Stiftung 24.) [Cf. 399.]

1054 La sfida del mondo povero. [Orig. title: The Challenge of World Poverty. Trad. by] Lia Volpatti. Milano, Il Saggiatore, 1976, 437 pp. [Cf. 739e.]

1055 Viśva nirdhantā kī cunautī. Hindi transl. of The Challenge of World Poverty by Mahendra Bharādvāj. Dillī & Patnā, Rājkamal Prakāśan, 1976, 445 pp. [Cf. 739e.]

1056 Was ist "politische Ökonomie"? [Orig. title: What is Political Economy?] Transl. by Fred Prager. (Wirtschaft und Gesellschaft 2 (1976): 1, pp. 13—20.) [Cf. 1038, 1088, 1125.]

1057 A Worried America. New York, Lutheran Council in the USA, 1976, 21 pp. [Cf. 1073.]
Address given at the 10th Annual Meeting of the Lutheran Council in the USA, March 11, 1976, in Philadelphia.

1058 [Afterword to:] Sjögren, Per: Den okände Gunnar Myrdal. [The Unknown Gunnar Myrdal.] (Dagens Nyheter 25/7 1976.)

1059 Friedman bär själv skuld till den växande kritiken. [Fried-

man Himself Is to Blame for the Growing Criticism.]
(Dagens Nyheter 28/12 1976.)

Reply to Erik Lundberg who was interviewed in Dagens Nyheter December 15, 1976, with reference to the article: Jag borde ha avböjt mitt eget pris i ekonomi (1060).

1060 Jag borde ha avböjt mitt eget pris i ekonomi. [I Should Not Have Accepted My Own Prize in Economic Science.] (Dagens Nyheter 14/12 1976.) [Cf. 1070.]

1061 Gunnar Myrdal kommenterar socialdemokratins valnederlag: "Nu måste vi tala om för svenska folket vad *vår* socialism är!" [Gunnar Myrdal Comments on the Social Democrats' Defeat in the Elections: "Now We Have to Tell the Swedish People What *Our* Socialism Is!"] (LO-tidningen 56 (1976): 26, pp. 6—7.)

Interview by Lena Askling and Elon Johanson.

1062 Relying on Human Goodness. (The Times 19/7 1976.)

Interview by Paul Harrison.

1977

1063 Asian Drama. An Inquiry Into the Poverty of Nations. An Abridgement of The Twentieth Century Fund Study by Seth King. [Foreword by M. J. Rossant.] Harmondsworth, Penguin Books, 1977, 388 pp. (Pelican Books.) [Cf. 786, 848.]

1064 Ett bra land som borde kunnat vara mycket bättre. [A Good Country Which Ought to Have Been Much Better.] (Ekonomisk debatt och ekonomisk politik. Ed. by Jan Herin and Lars Werin. Nationalekonomiska föreningen 100 år. Stockholm, Norstedt, 1977, pp. 235—48.)

1065 Contra a corrente. Ensaios críticos em economia. [Orig. title: Against the Stream. Critical Essays on Economics.] Trad. Heloisa Mendes Fortes de Oliveira. Rio de Janeiro, Campus, 1977, 303 pp. [Cf. 896c.]

1066 Dhārā ke viruddh. Hindi transl. of Against the Stream by Mahendra Bharādvāj. Dillī & Patnā, Rājkamal Prakāśan, 1977, 292 pp. [Cf. 896c.]

1067 Genmäle till Jan-Erik Lane. [Rebuttal to Jan-Erik Lane.] (Statsvetenskaplig tidskrift 80 (1977): 1, p. 29.)
Reply to Lane's article: Om Gunnar Myrdals värdepremissteori [On Gunnar Myrdal's Theory of Values], pp. 25—28.

1068 Lysande utsikter för ekonomisk forskning. [Splendid Outlook for Research in Economics.] (Ekonomisk debatt 5 (1977): 1, pp. 5—10.)

1069 The Meaning and Validity of Institutional Economics. (Economics in Institutional Perspective. Essays in Honor of K. William Kapp. Ed. by Rolf Steppacher . . . Lexington, Mass., 1977, pp. 3—10.) [Cf. 1030.]

1070 The Nobel Prize in Economic Science. (Challenge 20 (1977): 1, pp. 50—52.)
Transl. from an article in Dagens Nyheter 14/12 1976 (1060).

1071 Pin'gon-ŭi tojŏn. (Kaesŏl) Segye pin'gon ch'ubang p'ŭrogŭraem. [Korean transl. of] The Challenge of World Poverty [by] Ch'oe Kwang-nyŏl. Seoul, Hyŏnam sa, 1977, 508 pp. [Cf. 739e.]

1072 The Secret Vice. [Author's orig. title: Poverty in the Western Developed Countries.] (Ceres 10 (1977): 4, pp. 37—39.) [Cf. 1103.]

1073 A Worried America. (The Christian Century 94 (1977): 41, pp. 161—66.)
Adapted from Address delivered at the 10th Annual Meeting of the Lutheran Council in the USA (1057).

1978

1074 Behovet av reformer i underutvecklade länder. [Orig. title: Need for Reforms in Underdeveloped Countries.] Transl. into Swedish [from the author's English MS] by Olof Hoffsten. Stockholm, Utrikespolitiska Institutet, 1978, 32 pp. (Världspolitikens dagsfrågor 1978: 10.) [Cf. 1100, 1113, 1117.]

1075 Dags för ett bättre skattesystem! [Time for a Better Tax

System!] (Ekonomisk debatt 6 (1978): 7, pp. 493—506.) [Cf. 1112.]

1076 Educational Reform in Underdeveloped Countries. (The Social Context of Education. Essays in Honour of J. P. Naik. Ed. by A. B. Shah. Bombay, Allied, cop. 1978, pp. 68—75.) [Cf. 1023.]

1077 The Energy Crisis and International Cooperation. (Challenge 21 (1978): 1, pp. 65—67.)
Excerpt from the Félix Neubergh lecture at Gothenburg University, Sweden, October 21, 1977 (1079).

1078 In Memoriam: Egon Glesinger's Contribution to International Forestry and FAO. (Unasylva 30 (1978): 122, pp. 39—40.)

1079 Increasing Interdependence Between States but Failure of International Cooperation. Gothenburg, Gothenburg Univ., 1978, 53 pp. [Cf. 1098.]
The first Félix Neubergh lecture at Gothenburg University in October, 1977.

1080 Institutional Economics. (Journal of Economic Issues 12 (1978): 4, pp. 771—83.) — IIES Reprint Series 107. Stockholm, 1978. [Cf. 1099.]
Lecture presented at the University of Wisconsin, Madison, 15 Dec., 1977.

1081 An International Economy. Problems and Prospects. Westport, Conn., Greenwood Press, 1978, 381 pp.
Repr. of the ed., New York, 1956 (243).

1082 Un parallèle: le Front populaire (1936, le premier gouvernement Blum). [Orig. title: A Parallel: The First Blum Government 1936. A Footnote to History.] (Solutions socialistes: À propos de "La transition socialiste". Ed. Serge-Christophe Kolm. Paris, Editions Ramsay, 1978, pp. 143—46.) [Cf. 1119.]

1083 Political and Institutional Economics. Eleventh Geary Lecture, 1978. Dublin, The Economic and Social Research Institute, [1978], 15 pp.

1084 Politisches Manifest über die Armut in der Welt. [Orig. title:] The Challenge of World Poverty. Aus dem Amerikanischen von Suzanne Reichstein. Gekürzte Ausg. Die Bearb. besorgte Ernst-Josef Pauw. 3. Aufl. Frankfurt am Main, 1978, 284 pp. (Suhrkamp Taschenbuch 40.) [Cf. 864.]

1085 Procès de la croissance. A contre-courant. [Orig. title: Against the Stream.] Trad. de l'americain par TRADECOM. Paris, Presses universitaires, 1978, 278 pp. (Economie d'aujourd'hui.) [Cf. 896c.]

1086 Race and Class in a Welfare State. (The National Purpose Reconsidered. Ed. by Dona Baron. New York, Columbia University Press, 1978.) [Cf. 1104.]
Lecture at a symposium October 28, 1976, at Columbia University, New York.— Abbreviated version.

1087 Ulighed og underudvikling. [Inequality and Underdevelopment.] Overs. og red. [Transl. and ed.]: Niels Viderø. 2. oplag. København, Mellemfolkeligt samvirke, 1978, 72 pp. [Cf. 964.]

1088 What is Political Economy? (Dynamics of Development. An International Perspective. [Essays in Honour of J.N. Khosla.] Ed. by S.K. Sharma. Delhi, Concept Publ. Co., 1978, I, pp. 47—53.) [Cf. 1038, 1056, 1088.]

1089 De styrande säger nej — inte vanligt folk. [Leadership — Not the Common Man — Says No.] (Vestmanlands Läns Tidning 30/12 1978.)
Interview by Anders H. Pers.

1090 Grattis, Gunnar Myrdal, 80: men själv pratar han helst om toppstyrningen i partiet. [Happy Birthday, Gunnar Myrdal, 80, Who Prefers to Talk About the Oligarchy Within the Party.] (Aftonbladet 5/12 1978.)
Interview by Ronny Nygren.

1091 Ideals vs. Reality: Examining U.S. Social Policies in an

Interview With the Myrdals. (Part I.) (The Daily Texan Feb. 2, 1978.)

Interview by Harvey Neville.

1092 Sluta kohandla! Riv systemet! [Stop Horse-Trading! Tear Down the System!] (Dagens Nyheter 3/12 1978.)

Interview by Per Sjögren.

1093 Striving for Peace: Looking at the World, Its Problems and Future, with Two Dedicated Servants of Mankind. (Part II.) (The Daily Texan Feb. 3, 1978.)

Interview by Harvey Neville.

1979

1094 The Equality Issue in World Development. (1095: Essays and Lectures After 1975, pp. 1—22.) [Cf. 1025.]

1095 Essays and Lectures After 1975. [Ed. by Mutsumi Okada. Kyoto, Keibunsha, 1979], 175 pp.

Contents: The Equality Issue in World Development. (1094) — Peace Research and the Peace Movement. (1102) — Race and Class in a Welfare State. (1104) — Poverty in the Western Developed Countries. (1103) — Increasing Interdependence Between States but Failure of International Cooperation. (1098) — Institutional Economics. (1099) — Opening Statement. The Tom Slick Colloquium . . . March 10, 1978. (1101) — Need for Reforms in Underdeveloped Countries. (1100)

Volume includes Alva Myrdal: The Road to Peace: Obstacles and Opportunities. The Tom Slick Colloquium . . . March 10, 1978, pp. 127—36.

1096 Genmäle till Marcus Wallenberg med anledning av artikeln Några reflektioner kring efterkrigstidens ekonomiska politik i Sverige. [Rejoinder to Marcus Wallenberg: Reflections on Post-War Economic Policy in Sweden.] (Skandinaviska Enskilda Banken Kvartalsskrift 8 (1979): 3—4, pp. 66—71.) [Cf. 1105.]

1097 Hur får vi en skattedebatt som bär framåt? [How Can We Get a Tax Debate that Moves Forward?] (Tiden 71 (1979): 1, pp. 6—12.)

Reply to Gunnar Sträng: Nya problem kräver nya program — inte minst inom skattepolitiken. [New Problems Require New Programs — Not Least in Tax Politics.] (Tiden 70 (1978): 9—10, pp. 516—22.)

1098 Increasing Interdependence Between States but Failure of International Cooperation. (1095: Essays and Lectures After 1975, pp. 79—101.) [Cf. 1079.]

1099 Institutional Economics. (1095: Essays and Lectures After 1975, pp. 103—16.) [Cf. 1080.]

1100 Need for Reforms in Underdeveloped Countries. (1095: Essays and Lectures After 1975, pp. 137—60.) — Quarterly Economic Journal 6 (1979): 1, pp. 25—40. [Cf. 1113, 1117.]

1101 Opening Statement. The Tom Slick Colloquium . . . March 10, 1978. (1095: Essays and Lectures After 1975, pp. 117—26.)
Address given at the University of Texas, Austin.

1102 Peace Research and the Peace Movement. (1095: Essays and Lectures After 1975, pp. 23—33.) [Cf. 997[1].]

1103 Poverty in the Western Developed Countries. (1095: Essays and Lectures After 1975, pp. 71—78.) [Cf. 1072.]

1104 Race and Class in a Welfare State. Introductory Lecture to a Symposium in a Series Entitled "The National Purpose Reconsidered" 1776—1976 at Columbia University, October 28, 1976. (1095: Essays and Lectures After 1975, pp. 35—70.) — Mondes en développement 26 (1979), pp. 173—210. [Cf. 1086.]
With a résumé in French and Spanish in Mondes en développement.

1105 Rejoinder to Marcus Wallenberg with Reference to the Article: Reflections on Post-War Economic Policy in Sweden. (Skandinaviska Enskilda Banken Quarterly Review 8 (1979): 3—4, pp. 66—71.)
English transl. of (1096).

1106 Underdevelopment and the Evolutionary Imperative. (Third World Quarterly 1 (1979): 2, pp. 24—42.)

1107 Vi behöver mer av verklig dialog med politikerna. [We

Need Better Communication With the Politicians.] (LO-tidningen 59 (1979): 13, p. 3.)

- - - - - - - - - -

1108 Promsen är ingen nyhet. [The 'Proms' is Nothing New.] (Svenska Dagbladet 2/3 1979.)

1109 Gospodarka i polityka. [Economy and Politics.] (Glos 3 (1979): 15, pp. 11—15.)

1980

1110 Asiatisches Drama. Eine Untersuchung über die Armut der Nationen. Eine Studie des Twentieth Century Fund in der Kurzfassung von Seth S. King. [Orig. title: Asian Drama . . . Aus dem Englischen von Nils Lindquist.] 1. Aufl. Frankfurt am Main, Suhrkamp, 1980, 447 pp. (Suhrkamp Taschenbuch 634.) [Cf. 900.]

1111 Contra la corriente. Ensayos críticos sobre economía. [Orig. title: Against the Stream. Critical Essays on Economics.] Trad. de Xavier Calsamiglia y Mariona Costa. 1. ed. Barcelona, Ariel, 1980, 383 pp. (Demos. Biblioteca de ciencia económica.) [Cf. 896c.]

1112 Gedanken zu einer Reform des Steuersystems. [Orig. title: Dags för ett bättre skattesystem!] (Wirtschaft und Gesellschaft 6 (1980): 4, pp. 349—66.) [Cf. 1075.]

1113 Need for Reforms in Underdeveloped Countries. (Twenty-First Century. Prospects and Problems. Ed. Kee Hyong Kim. Seoul, Kyung Hee University Press, 1980, pp. 87—109.) [Cf. 1100, 1117.]
Lecture at The Joint International Symposium of The Club of Rome and The Center for the Reconstruction of Human Society, October 29—31, 1979, Kyung Hee University, Seoul.

1114 Nödhjälp i stället för utvecklingsbistånd. [Relief Instead of Development Aid.] (Ekonomisk debatt 8 (1980): 8, pp. 565—69.) [Cf. 1120.]

1115 The Crisis of the Swedish Welfare State. (Challenge 23 (1980): 3, pp. 38—41.)
Interview by Bertram Silverman.

1981

1116 L'elemento politico nello sviluppo della teoria economica. [Orig. title: Vetenskap och politik i nationalekonomien.] Transl. [from the English The Political Element in the Development of Economic Theory] into Italian by Pier Luigi Cecioni. Firenze, Sansoni Editore, 1981, 261 pp. [Cf. 11c, 826.]

1117 Need for Reforms in Underdeveloped Countries. (The World Economic Order. Past and Prospects. Ed. by Sven Grassman and Erik Lundberg. London, Macmillan, 1981, pp. 501—25.) — IIES Reprint Series 161. Stockholm, 1981. [Cf. 1100, 1113.]
Lecture at symposium, August 25—28, 1978, at Saltsjöbaden, Sweden.

1118 Nödhjälp i stället för utvecklingshjälp. [Relief Instead of Development Aid.] (Ekonomisk debatt 9 (1981): 4, pp. 292—95.)
Reply to comments elicited by Nödhjälp i stället för utvecklingsbistånd (1114).

1119 A Parallel: The First Blum Government 1936. A Footnote to History. (Studies in Economic Theory and Practice. Essays in Honour of Edward Lipiński. Ed. by N. Assorodobraj-Kula . . . Amsterdam, North Holland, 1981, pp. 53—62.) [Cf. 1082.]

1120 Relief Instead of Development Aid. [Orig. title: Nödhjälp i stället för utvecklingsbistånd.] (Intereconomics 16 (1981): 2, pp. 86—89.) [Cf. 1114.]

1121 Alf Johansson död. [Alf Johansson In Memoriam.] (Dagens Nyheter 20/2 1981.)
Obituary.

Among forthcoming publications

1122 Fines y medios en política económica. [Orig. title: Das Zweck-Mittel-Denken in der Nationalökonomie.] Madrid. (Libros de Bolsillo.) [Cf. 42, 299.]

1123 Hur styrs landet? [How Is the Country Governed?] Stockholm, Rabén & Sjögren.

1124 Political Economy and Institutional v. Conventional Economics. (Samuelson and Neoclassical Economics. Ed. by George R. Feiwel. Boston, Martinus Nijhoff, 1981.)

1125 What is Political Economy? (Value Judgement and Income Distribution. Ed. by Robert A. Solo and Charles W. Anderson. New York, Praeger, 1981.) [Cf. 1038, 1056, 1088.]

Addenda

A1 Arbetslösheten och dess behandling. [Unemployment and Its Remedy.] (Nationalekonomiska Föreningens Förhandlingar 12 okt. 1931 [pr. 1932], pp. 105—11.)
Rebuttal at the meeting of the Society of Political Economy (Stockholm), October 12, 1931.

A2 Planhushållning. [Planned Economy.] (Nationalekonomiska Föreningens Förhandlingar 20 nov. 1934, pp. 167—75, 200—01.)
Rebuttal at the meeting of the Society of Political Economy (Stockholm), November 20, 1934.

A3 Bostadsbehov och bostadsbyggande. [The Need for Housing and the Building of Housing.] (Nationalekonomiska Föreningens Förhandlingar 9 maj 1935 [pr. 1936], pp. 109—12, 116—17.)
Rebuttal at the meeting of the Society of Political Economy (Stockholm), May 9, 1935.

A4 Om försörjningsplikt mot föräldrar och befolkningskommissionens förslag. [On the Duty to Take Care of One's

Parents and the Population Commission's Proposition.]
(SAP Information 1936:4, pp. 77—78.)
Reply prompted by an enquiry to SAP Information.

A5   U.S.A. kommer med: Inställningen radikalt omsvängd.
       Isolationismen dog den 9 april. [The U.S.A. to Join: Opin-
       ion Radically Changed. Isolationism Died on April 9.]
       (Dagens Nyheter 28/5 1940.)
       Interview by Bertil Arborén (signed Bert).

A6   Det internationella uppbyggnadsproblemet. [The Interna-
       tional Problem of Reconstruction.] (Morgon-Tidningen/
       Social Demokraten 6/3 1943.) [Cf. 118, 136.]

A7   * Betänkande den 4 oktober 1944 angående investeringsav-
       vägningen. [Report October 4, 1944, on the Deliberation of
       Investment.] [With] Ingvar Svennilson. Stockholm, 1944,
       pp. 73—90. (SOU 1944: 57. Finansdepartementet.
       Framställningar och utlåtanden från Kommissionen för
       ekonomisk efterkrigsplanering.)

A8   * Betänkande den 4 oktober 1944 angående kontantun-
       derstöd och dagunderstöd till arbetslösa m.m. [Report
       October 4, 1944, on Unemployment Benefits, etc.] [With]
       Richard Sterner. Stockholm, 1944, pp. 109—34. (SOU
       1944: 57.)

A9   * Betänkande den 27 september 1944 angående produktion
       på lager. [Report September 27, 1944, on Production in
       Stock.] [With] Arne Björnberg. Stockholm, 1944, pp. 41—
       50. (SOU 1944: 57.)

A10   Efterkrigsplaneringen. [Post-War Planning.] (SAP Infor-
       mation 1944: 23—24, pp. 345—46.)

A11   * Utlåtande den 10 maj 1944 över investeringsutredningens
       betänkande den 3 april 1944 med förslag till inves-
       teringsreserv m.m. [Statement May 10, 1944, on the Invest-
       ment Commission Report of April 3, 1944 . . .] [With] Arne
       Björnberg. Stockholm, 1944, pp. 21—33. (SOU 1944: 57.)

147

A12 * Utlåtande den 26 april 1944 över fullmäktiges i riksbanken skrivelse den 30 mars 1944 angående riktlinjer för den statliga penningpolitiken. [Statement April 26, 1944, on the Guiding Principles for Government Monetary Policy . . .] [With] Karin Kock. Stockholm, 1944, pp. 7—19. (SOU 1944: 57.)

A13 Inflation eller socialism. [Inflation or Socialism.] (Morgon-Tidningen 27/9 1944.) [Cf. 134.]
Lecture to a Trade Union Meeting in Stockholm, September 26, 1944.

A14 Min negerbok begriper bara vetenskapsmän. [Only the Professionals Understand My Book on the Negroes.] (Dagens Nyheter 31/1 1944.)
Interview by Alma Braathen (signed Brodjaga).

A15 Tidens industrikritik. [Industrial Criticism in Tiden.] (Tiden 37 (1945), pp. 107—15.)

A16 På fredens tröskel: Ökad inflationspress, arbetsfred nödvändig. [On the Threshold of Peace: Increased Pressure for Inflation, Labor Settlement Necessary.] (Dagens Nyheter 14/1 1945.)
Interview.

A17 Handelspolitiken och krediterna. [Trade Policy and Credit.] (Morgon-Tidningen 6/4 1947.)

A18 The United Nations Economic Commission for Europe as an Organ of All-European Economic Cooperation. Lecture given under the auspices of the Institute of Economics of the Academy of Sciences of the USSR at the Lomonosov State University of Moscow, 9 March, 1956. 14 pp. [Stencil.]

A19 Myrdal utreder ekonomiproblem i Sydöstasien. [Myrdal Investigates Economic Problems in Southeast Asia.] (Svenska Dagbladet 19/12 1957.)
Interview by Allan Hernelius.

A20   Striden om ryssavtalet spelas upp igen: 'Tingsten tänkte inte med hjärnan.' [The Fight Over the Russian Trade Agreement is Re-enacted: 'Tingsten Did Not Think With His Brain'.] (Dagens Nyheter 19/8 1963.)

Reply to Herbert Tingsten: Mitt liv [My Life], III, Stockholm, Norstedt, 1963, pp. 126—39.

A21   Myrdal i amerikansk radiointervju: USA saknar rätta organisationer för effektiv arbetsmarknadspolitik. [Myrdal in American Radio Interview: the US Lacks Proper Organizations for Effective Labor Policy.] (Svenska Dagbladet 1/7 1964.) [Cf. A22.]

Swedish transl. of interview made by Barry Farber for the WOR radio network, New York.

A22   Well-Known Capitalist Economist Dr. Myrdal. (The American Swedish Monthly 58 (1964): 7, pp. 12—13.) [Cf. A21.]

Transcription of a small part of an interview made by Barry Farber for the WOR radio network, New York.

A23   The Negro and the Democratic Ideal of Equality. (The Negro Struggle for Equality in the Twentieth Century. William C. Ames. Lexington, Mass., D.C. Heath and Co., cop. 1965, pp. 2—5.) (New Dimensions in American History.)

From An American Dilemma, New York, Harpers, 1944, pp. 3—5, 24.

A24   [Foreword to:] Geōrgia kai oikonomikē anaptyxis. [Greek transl. of Priorities in the Development Efforts of Underdeveloped Countries and Their Trade and Financial Relations with Rich Countries.] Organismos trophōn kai geōrgias (FAO). Athēnai, Argyrēs Papazēzēs, [1965], pp. 9—30. (Themata oikonomikēs anaptyxeōs 4.) [Cf. 427.]

A25   Europas ekonomiska splittring ett svårt amerikanskt nederlag. [Europe's Economic Division, a Severe American Setback.] (Företagsekonomi 33 (45) (1966): 6, pp. 226, 228—29.) [Cf. 529.]

Excerpts from lecture at UCLA, May 4, 1966: The United States and the Integration Endeavors in Europe.

A26 Jag tror på USA:s förmåga att lösa rasproblemet. [I Believe in the United States' Capability to Solve the Racial Problem.] (Expressen 9/4 1968.) [Cf. A27.]

Telephone interview by Robert J. Donovan. — On the situation in the United States after the murder of Martin Luther King.

A27 Myrdal Fears Assassination Tradition Will Arise in U.S. (Los Angeles Times 9/4 1968.) [Cf. A26.]

Interview by Robert J. Donovan.

A28 Kan vi hjälpa de underutvecklade länderna? [Can We Help the Underdeveloped Countries?] (Ansvar 17 (1970): 4, pp. 40—42.)

Summary of a lecture in Stockholm, October 24—25, 1970.

A29 [Statement during the] Hearings Before the Ad Hoc Subcommittee on Urban Growth of the Committee on Banking and Currency, House of Representatives, Ninety-First Congress, First and Second Sessions on The Quality of Urban Life. Part 2. Washington D.C., U.S. Govt. Printing Office, 1970, pp. 304—34.

A30 Professor Gunnar Myrdal Returns to the South. (Time 23/11 1970.)

Interview by Karsten Prager.

A31 To politiko stoicheio stēn oikonomikē theōria. [Orig. title:] The Political Element in the Development of Economic Theory. Metaphrasē K. M. Sophoulē. [With author's new Preface.] Athēnai, Ekdoseis Papazēsē, 1971, 333 pp. (Seira Epistēmē kai koinōnia.) [Cf. 11c.]

A32 Gunnar Myrdal efter TV-grälet med Benne Lantz: Jag sa bara högt vad andra tänker. [Gunnar Myrdal After the TV Discussion With Benne Lantz: I Just Said What Others Are Thinking.] (Aftonbladet 7/2 1971.)

Interview by Renée Höglin.

A33 Hyŏndae pokchi kukkaron. [Korean transl. of Beyond the Welfare State.] See (A34).

A34   Kyŏngje iron-gwa chŏgaebal chiyŏk. [Korean transl. of] Economic Theory and Underdeveloped Regions [by] Ch'oe Kwang-nyŏl. — Hyŏndae pokchi kukkaron. [Korean transl. of Beyond the Welfare State [by] Ch'oe Kwang-nyŏl. Seoul, Changmun'gak, 1972, 548 pp. (Hyŏndae kyŏngje kyŏngyŏng ch'ongsŏ 9.) [Cf. 255e, 323e.]

A35   Kyŏngje haksŏl-kwa chŏngch'ijŏk yoso. [Korean transl. of] The Political Element in the Development of Economic Theory] [by] Ch'oe Kwang-nyŏl. Seoul, Changmun'gak, 1974, 362 pp. (K. G. Myrdal-ŭi kyŏngje sasang-gwa pokchi sahoeron 7.) [Cf. 11c.]

A36   P'ungyo-eŭi chojaeng. [Korean transl. of] Challenge to Affluence [by] Ch'oe Kwang-nyŏl. Seoul, Changmun'gak, 1974, 243 pp. (K. G. Myrdal-ŭi kyŏngje sasang-gwa pokchi sahoeron 5.) [Cf. 387c.]

A37   Fredsforskningen bör arbeta med de aktuella kriserna. Får inte förfalla till teoretiska modellbyggen. [Peace Research. Focus on the Present Crises and Not on Theoretical Models.] (Arbetaren 53 (1974): 51—52, pp. 8—9.)

A38   Myrdal: Poor Planning Saps U.S. Economy. (The National Observer, Dec. 7, 1974.)
Interview by William J. Lanouette.

INDEX

The titles of the author's own works are in italics
The letters *ü, å, ä* and *ö* are alphabetized as if they had no marks, i.e. as *u, a, a,* and o.
Interviews are denoted by (I) after the title.

153

163